# Candymaking in Canada

# Candymaking in Canada

## The History and Business of Canada's Confectionery Industry

David Carr

THE DUNDURN GROUP
TORONTO

Editor: Andrea Pruss
Design: Emma Kassirer
Printer: University of Toronto Press

**National Library of Canada Cataloguing in Publication Data**

Carr, David, 1940-
    Candymaking in Canada / David Carr.

Includes bibliographical references and index.

ISBN 1-55002-395-0

1. Chocolate candy — Canada.  2. Candy industry — Canada.  I. Title.

HD9330.C653C65 2002        338.4'7664153'0971        C2002-902293-2

1   2   3   4   5        07   06   05   04   03

We acknowledge the support of the **Canada Council for the Arts** and the **Ontario Arts Council** for our publishing program. We also acknowledge the financial support of the **Government of Canada** through the **Book Publishing Industry Development Program** and **The Association for the Export of Canadian Books**, and the **Government of Ontario** through the **Ontario Book Publishers Tax Credit** program, and the **Ontario Media Development Corporation's Ontario Book Initiative.**

Care has been taken to trace the ownership of copyright material used in this book. The author and the publisher welcome any information enabling them to rectify any references or credit in subsequent editions.

                              *J. Kirk Howard, President*

Printed and bound in Canada.⊕
Printed on recycled paper.
www.dundurn.com

Except where noted, permission to reprint photographs was obtained from the following:

All photographs of Nestlé products, personnel, machinery, advertising, etc., including "After Eight" and "Rowntree" brands, courtesy of Nestlé Canada Inc.
All photographs of Neilson's products, personnel, machinery, advertising, etc., including "No-Name" and "Cadbury" brands, courtesy of William Neilson Ltd. / Ltée.

Dundurn Press
8 Market Street
Suite 200
Toronto, Ontario, Canada
M5E 1M6

Dundurn Press
2250 Military Road
Tonawanda NY
U.S.A. 14150

# Candymaking in Canada

# Table of Contents

*To Mom and Dad*

# Acknowledgements

**Within** hours of the good people at Dundurn giving the go-ahead for this book I was in my local telling a number of friends about the project for the first time. For two hours the table was consumed with talk of favourite candies both past and present. The conversation and the enthusiasm in which it was conducted signalled I was on the right track.

Writing your first real book (I had previously done an in-house publication for a client) is a longer journey than one thinks. It encompasses not only those who help you from start to finish, but also those who supported you long before the first advance cheque. They are not always the same people, but they should be recognized nevertheless.

It is incredible the number of friends and family members who have stepped up to the plate. Susan Puff and Ross Lewchuk, who weave their special magic in anything I take on. Norma Bishop and Ted Raspin, who selflessly gave time on this particular project no matter when I called, or what I needed. Chris Hernandez, who was available when the computer forgot to do what computers do and it looked like chunks of manuscript may have been lost.

I would also like to thank friends like Stuart Irvine, Peter McLarty, Carol Manwell and Scott Turner, who have worked hard on projects that never came together, and remain a foundation for the one that finally has.

Then there is the book itself. A large number of candy-makers came forward to help with this project, and have been patient while I raided their archives and have held on to their precious photographs. These people provided me with raw material that, like chocolate or candy, had to be molded. And for that I offer special thanks.

One final note. The history of chocolate and candy is a story of many conflicting dates and time frames (sometimes from the same source). I have done my best to ensure accuracy, but accept full responsibility for any errors contained in this book.

# Section I

# Letter From the Candy Counter

Selecting a snack treat is not what it used to be. At the corner store, chocolate and candy are two islands in a sea of tempting alternatives that has expanded from potato chips and ice cream to include individual packages of cookies and crackers.

The total candy market in Canada, including chocolate bars, boxed chocolates, cough drops, candied breath mints, and non-chocolate confections, is $2.3 billion. And what do we get in return for our money?

Chocolate continues to dominate the candy counter, with close to 50 percent of the market. The bulk of those sales have been described by one European-based chocolate society as a "low-grade, cloying confection." The difference between low-grade and high-grade chocolate is the amount of cocoa butter introduced into the recipe. The higher the butter count, the better the chocolate. Or so say the experts.

Neilson's dominated the candy counter, as this photograph shows. Still, there are packaging examples of other products, including Rolo, Biscrisp, Caramilk, Aero, Sweet Marie, Caravan, Kit Kat, Coffee Crisp, Smarties, Raisins, Milky Way, and Turkish Delight.

11

Most Canadians appear to think differently. Last year, on average, we gobbled up approximately twenty-five pounds of chocolate. Kit Kat remains the perennial favourite, with Coffee Crisp, Oh Henry, Smarties, Caramilk, Reese Peanut Butter Cups, Aero, the original Mars bar, Wunder Bar, and Mr. Big routinely rounding out the top ten. Interestingly, Snickers, which usually finishes in the top three in the United States, ranked eleventh in Canada at last count.

Also of interest is the fact that only one in ten chocolate bars lasts for very long in the marketplace. Five of the bars on that list have been around since before the Second World War — all but two since the 1960s.

Manufacturers have been trying to improve the odds of new products by putting a new twist on favourite brands, either permanently or as so-called special editions. Hence chunky Kit Kat and Aero, and the addition of orange flavouring in bars such as Coffee Crisp and Crunchie (whose parent, Cadbury, owns Crush brand soft drinks). The trend has continued into the freezer, where we can routinely purchase ice cream versions of our favourite chocolate treats.

Meanwhile, Canada's taste in chocolate is changing, as more Canadians are willing to either put to one side or complement our traditional preference for milk chocolate in favour of darker varieties.

John Lebel, an assistant professor of marketing at Concordia University's John Molson School of Business, attributes this first change in twenty years to Michel Montignac, a French physician who, like his seventeenth-century predecessor, is trying to promote the healthier aspects of dark chocolate — at least where comparisons are concerned. (Of course, Dr. Montignac has his own line of dark chocolate, so his motives can be questioned, even if the success of his message cannot.)

Preferences in chocolate, as well as in candy, were once strongly defined by regional tastes. In Quebec, the sweeter the better. Smiles and Chuckles' Turkish Delight would fly off the shelves in Newfoundland, though not in other parts of Canada. Today, 80 percent of candy is universal within the Canadian market.

But regional differences in taste still remain. French Canadians are more adventurous and have created a vibrant new market for traditional recipes like dark chocolate mixed with green peppercorns. Chocolate lovers from Quebec are also more interested in matching chocolate with wine.

Even with such regional exceptions, variations in taste now travel along age and gender rather than geographic lines. How so? Males account for no more than 35 percent of chocolate consumption. At least we've moved male consumption out of the closet. Take, for example, an article about The Demon Candy that appeared in the September 1910 issue of *The Atlantic Monthly*, describing men as secretive chocolate consumers:

> It was probably true that children and females consumed the bulk of [chocolate], although secret candy-eating may even at that time have been in its incipiency among the fathers of a generation that still consumes its confectionery with a certain unpleasant reticence.

It was Jean Harlow, not John Barrymore, who bit into a piece of chocolate in the 1933 comedy classic *Dinner at Eight*, thus showcasing the simple indulgence on the silver screen for the first time. Harlow was probably enjoying a piece of milk chocolate. "Women tend to prefer milk chocolate," says Leber. "However, as they age, they begin to acquire a taste for darker chocolate."

Boxed chocolates continue to be popular, although the market has altered significantly. Young men no longer feel the pressure to impress (some would say bribe) the mother by arriving at the door with a fancy selection when taking out the daughter for the first time.

Today, the biggest boxed chocolate occasions are Valentine's Day, Easter, and Mother's Day. These three account for 80 percent of boxed chocolate sales (though the major grocery store down the street sells a whopping 70 percent of its chocolate boxes just at Christmas). The rest of the year, manufacturers "eat their profits," says Lebel.

One part of the chocolate industry unlikely to change remains our resistance to low-fat varieties, as evidenced by the short-lived Crispy Crunch Light. It would appear that once we have decided upon a treat, we have already crossed the calorie threshold. A chocolate bar with 33 percent less fat is not going to make a difference. Why should it? Although with recent obesity red flags and the noticeable switch to dark chocolate, the day may come when it does.

What is certain on both sides of the candy counter is that while our appetite for confections continues to grow, the number of companies feeding that hunger will continue to shrink. In 1961, Canada had 194 plants in production. Today, we have fewer than 94. The major cause has been consolidation and the phasing out of smaller, obsolete production facilities. Some of those that have melted away were once located in the heart of major Canadian cities, housing operations in magnificent turn-of-the-twentieth-century brick factories.

The convergence of chocolate and non-chocolate brands has also contributed to the sunset. Sugar is popular again, and this time chocolate manufacturers are refusing to sit on the sidelines as Canadians flock to candy counters and recently opened candy stores to fill up on their favourite chocolates, sweets, and bags of nostalgic treats.

Canada's confectionery industry is anxious to cash in on the fastest growing segment of the confections business, changing the complexion of what was once a market dominated by faceless, independent suppliers of bubble gum, sours, and jellies (categories that the over thirty-five demographic may refer to as penny candy).

"It still is penny candy, but these days it's a penny a gram instead of a piece," jokes Jack Green, president of Toronto-based Retail Entertainment Inc., which owns Suckers, an interactive candy store that blends a wall of bulk confectionery bins with packaged brands and candy-related toys, music, and videos.

In an average week, Canadians drop as much as 600 million pennies ($60,000) at high volume candy stores. Other candy stores eschew the glitz of Suckers for a basic retail concept more reminiscent of the old-fashioned candy store.

Whether consumers go for high energy or stark wooden floors — or the candy counter at the corner store — it is the shelves that tell the story. And more shelf space is being handed over to branded sugar products.

"The competitive set is changing in the market," explains Paul Sullivan, vice-president of marketing for Cadbury Trebor Allan, a recent merger between Britain's Cadbury chocolate maker with Burlington, Ontario's Allan, Canada's largest supplier of five- to twenty-five-cent candy pieces (the so-called chunk or count goods segment). "Major branded players from chocolate are moving into the sugar side of the business and are bringing some of their branding techniques over."

Cadbury, which bought William Neilson Ltd., maker of domestic favourites such as Jersey Milk, Crispy Crunch, and Sweet Marie, is not alone. Other chocolate makers have moved into the sugar candy business, including American-based behemoths Mars (Skittles) and Hershey (hard-boiled candies and caramels), as well as Nestlé Canada, the Canadian subsidiary of Nestlé S.A., the global food giant based in Vevey, Switzerland, which also produces Kit Kat, Smarties, and Canada's own Coffee Crisp.

Nestlé purchased London, Ontario-based O'Pee Chee in 1997, rolling several licensed favourites like Sweet Tarts, Nerds, and purple Thrills chewing gum under its American Wonka brand.

"There is an increase in strong branding in the business," says a spokesperson for the Nestlé Wonka brand. "We're branding fun, and we're relying on established brands such as Nerds to capitalize on new trends." This includes a new line of Wonka gumballs with Nerds tucked inside.

It is a matter of growth potential, according to Cadbury Trebor Allan's Paul Sullivan. The sugar segment is exploding like Pop Rocks (a popular kid's confection that bursts inside the mouth). "Categories are harder to define in Canada, but you look at trends in the U.S. over the last five years and sugar has been growing at between eight and nine percent a year, while chocolate sales are flat."

Plus using sugar offers more to work with in terms of colours and shapes that appeal to the fickle core market of six- to nine-year-olds. Paul Cherrie, vice-president of Concord Confections agrees. "The price of entry used to be that the candy had to taste good. Now the candy has to actually do something."

Named after the southern Ontario region where it is based, Concord Confections bills itself as the world's largest manufacturer of gumballs. The company made North American headlines in 1990 when it purchased New York-based Fleer Confections from the financially troubled Marvel Entertainment Group, publisher of Spiderman comics. Fleer accidentally stumbled on the recipe for Dubble Bubble, the world's first bubble gum, in 1928.

"Until Dubble Bubble we didn't have a recognizable brand," admits Cherrie. "We had to scratch and claw our way into the market. We now have a trademark that took generations to build. Dubble Bubble is to bubble gum what Coca Cola is to soft drinks."

And is that important in a market that caters to the most fickle of all tastes?

Approximately 95 percent of Concord's market is in the United States. Interactive brands include Candy Blox, stackable sugar bricks with a taste similar to Wonka's Sweet Tarts. "If you place Candy Blox against Sweet Tarts, a kid is going to go for the Blox because of the play value," Cherrie says. And not just kids: several years ago, a Chicago architectural firm placed the single largest order for Candy Blox to present a sugar-based model of a building for a client. Sort of a Lego set that should be kept out of the rain.

Another attraction of sugar has been the low-cost approach to marketing. Pez, one of the original interactive candies, has never engaged in marketing since the company first introduced plastic dispensers to sell coloured candy bricks in the 1950s. Pez remains one of the industry's top sellers. "Sugar candy has been around forever and candy stores have been around forever," says Sean McCann, president of Sugar Mountain, another candy store chain with outlets in Toronto and Vancouver. "It's the candy that sells." Still, there are signs that this too is changing.

An estimated 250 new sugar products appear on store shelves every year. And recipes seem to call for more: more sour, more colourful, more interactive. More than 90 percent of the new entrants will disappear within two years. Novelty candies and candies linked to popular culture will dissolve even faster.

"There's always a risk with products tied to a movie or other piece of popular culture," a marketing representative at Topps points out. "But it can deliver a big bang if timed right." To reduce the risk, manufacturers such as Cadbury Trebor Allan will use licensees for promotional work as opposed to launching new products.

Cadbury Trebor Allan has used hockey legend Wayne Gretzky and basketball great Shaquille O'Neal to promote Mr. Big. More recently, the company used Toronto Raptors star Vince Carter to act as a spokesman for several brands in Canada and the United States, where the company sells approximately 40 percent of its candy.

There are also signs that Canada's sugar candy industry is taking marketing to the next level, which will include radio and television spots.

Werther's Original butterscotch drops was one of the first sugar confections to realize the potential of television. "Almost overnight they turned the candy into a huge brand with a big following," says Sullivan. "Television is the next step. In the U.S. most of the major companies have sugar confectionery advertising on TV."

And what are Canada's sugar candymakers likely to push? Suckers are enormous, according to Topps. That category has been redefined by the return of the Chupa Chup.

While kids will continue to drive the sale of sugar candy, the size of the retro market cannot be dismissed, although most candymakers insist it is the by-product of a healthy industry. "We don't target nostalgia," Nestlé's insists.

Concord's Paul Cherrie argues that as an overarching trend, the retro market will fade, but that should not hurt manufacturers with established brands. "Confectionery really is a category that transcends age barriers. Our core market does not remember what retro is."

# The History of Chocolate

_"If one swallows a cup of chocolate only three hours after a copious lunch, everything will be perfectly digested and there will still be room for dinner."_

Brillat Savarin

Colourfully wrapped chocolate bars line store candy displays. Ice-cold chocolate milk is stocked in supermarket refrigerators, while higher end chocolatiers such as Laura Secord and Godiva sell eight out of every ten fancy boxes of chocolates in the lead-up to Valentine's Day, Easter, and Mother's Day.

Chocolate is the world's favourite flavour. It is also one of the world's most global food products. Cultivated in the New World and transported to the Old, the chocolate we enjoy today has been influenced by over five centuries of innovation and refinement in many countries, including Spain, the Netherlands, Switzerland, and England — and, to a lesser extent, the United States and even Canada.

Yet the origins of chocolate are planted exclusively in the temperamental roots of the _Theobroma cacao_. The tree was named in 1753 by Swedish botanist Carl von Linné, who found the Old World's initial name for the plant, _cacao_, or chocolate tree, too vulgar. Von Linné preferred instead to respect the tree's New World roots by combining the Greek _theos_, or god, with _broma_, or beverage.[1]

Over the years, the Old World appears to have won out as the name _Theobroma cacao_ has been simplified to the more manageable "cacao tree." But the name is the only thing that is simple about this complex tree. To produce its harvest, the cacao tree must be grown in moist and humid climates, no further than twenty degrees longitude on either side of the equator.

The first known use of the cacao bean occurred in the fourth century, immediately south of present-day Mexico, amid the inspiring stone temple cities of what is often referred to as the Mayan empire. The empire can be more accurately described as a group of Mayan states, sharing a similar culture and little else, that stretched from the Yucatán peninsula to the Pacific coast of Guatemala.

The Mayan culture is widely considered to be the greatest civilization of the original cultures. Known as "people of the book," the Mayans could write of their art and culture, including the use of the valuable cacao bean.

"The bean was so highly valued, that it was used as a form of currency at a fixed market rate," wrote the *New Internationalist* in an in-depth feature on the cocoa chain. "You could get a rabbit for ten beans, a slave cost a hundred and a prostitute went from eight to ten according to how they agree."

The valuable cacao bean was also used by Mayan priests to create a thick spicy chocolate drink known as *chocolatl*. Cacao was considered to be a symbol of both fertility and prosperity. The "drink of the gods" produced from the bean was used to solemnize sacred rituals and was consumed by Mayan elite, who often contained their chocolate in magnificent pottery cylinders.

As with chocolate today, the Mayans did not have just one drink recipe. Ingredients such as porridge, gruel, and spices (including chili) were carefully added to create different tastes and textures.

The Mayans were also aggressive traders. As a result, chocolate had already spread north to the Aztec Empire of central Mexico by the time the Mayan civilization began to crumble in the ninth century. The frugal Aztecs used the cacao bean as currency, using beans to prepare *chocolatl* only when the commodity had become so worn that it could no longer be traded.

Once again, the consumption of chocolate was considered a luxury restricted to Aztec kings, noblemen, and the upper ranks of the priesthood, although chocolate was also given to warriors because of its energy-boosting properties.

According to American historian William Hickling, Emperor Montezuma of Mexico refused any beverage other than *chocolatl,* which he consumed in goblets before entering his harem, likely contributing to the belief that the drink was also an aphrodisiac. The Emperor is reported to have consumed up to 50 cups of *chocolatl* a day.

Christopher Columbus tasted the drink in 1502 but was largely unimpressed. Spanish explorer and conqueror Hernán Cortés was quick to recognize the value the Aztecs placed on cacao beans in 1519. He established cacao plantations around the Caribbean and returned to Spain in 1528 with a cargo of beans, an Aztec recipe, and the instruments for preparing the native drink.

*Chocolatl* predates the arrival of coffee and tea in Europe by more than eighty years. And it was in Spain that the drink would undergo its first major innovation. Early acceptance of the New World drink within the Spanish political and cultural elite was decidedly mixed. One individual described the bitter-tasting liquid as better fit for pigs than for people.

Nevertheless, enthusiasm for the beverage could not be contained, especially after the Spanish emperor sweetened the drink with cane sugar, vanilla, and even wine. For the next century, Spanish clergy would continue to refine the drink with nuts, powdered flowers, orange water, and recently discovered spices and sugar from the Orient.

Chocolate became a welcome addition to an otherwise bland diet of meat, bread, porridge, and a limited supply of vegetables. The Spanish were anxious to keep the exotic beverage a secret from the rest of Europe.

In 1580, the first chocolate-processing plant was established in Spain. By this time, chocolate was a status symbol to be enjoyed in excess by a privileged few. Initially, the drink was consumed in the original manner of the Mayans and the Aztecs. As the appetite for chocolate grew, the method of transferring the liquid from vessel to lip was refined. It was served thick, cold, and frothy in cups, and would later be poured hot from steaming gold vermeil carafes or chocolate pots.

Fashionable *Chocolateríes* became features in Spanish cities and towns. The wealthy would gather in the afternoon for a cup of chocolate and a piece of *picatoste*, or fried bread, to dip in it. Less fashionable was the rumour that Charles the Second of Spain sat sipping chocolate while observing victims of the inquisition being put to death.

The Spanish considered the properties of chocolate to be less spiritual and more medicinal. It was common for medical entrepreneurs to study the exotic substances brought back by explorers as a cure for various ailments. Chocolate was no exception, and it was said to be useful for covering up poisons.

By the late 1600s, the grand ladies of the land had become so fond of this frothy beverage that they were accustomed to having it served to them frequently, even in church. As justification for their enjoyment, they referred to its medicinal use, and claimed it prevented fainting and "weakness" during the long ceremonies.

One bishop considered it a blatant abuse, and he forbade the practice. Drinking chocolate in church obviously broke the fast laws. (Not to mention that so much pleasure must be pagan!) The ladies, in retaliation, simply took themselves and their entourage to another church. A rumour holds that the offending clergyman later died of a cup of poisoned chocolate. The whole affair became a fearful scandal.

Eventually, in 1662, Pope Alexander VII put a final solution to the affair when he declared "Liquidum non frangit jejunum." [Liquids (including chocolate) do not break the fast.] It is likely that this decision was based on the fact that chocolate, like so many other herbs, was considered to have medicinal qualities.

The pleasure of chocolate could not be contained. Word of this extraordinary beverage spread throughout Europe. Antonio Carletti, a Florentine merchant, wrote about the growing and processing of cacao into a drink during a visit to Guatemala.

The Spanish custom of chocolate drinking was introduced to the French court in 1615, during the marriage of Anne of Austria with Louis XIII of France. A gift of chocolate was part of the Spanish Infanta's dowry.

The French also seized on the medicinal properties of chocolate. Francois Joseph Broussais, a French physician born in 1772, said, "Chocolate of good quality, well made, properly cooked, is one of the best cures that I have yet found for my patients and for myself."

By the 1650s, approximately 130 years after *chocolatl* had been introduced to Spain, chocolate had made its way across the English Channel to London. It might have arrived much sooner, but Elizabethan privateers, patrolling the seas of the late sixteenth century for Spanish ships to plunder, appeared even less impressed by the cacao bean than Columbus.

In 1579, the English buccaneers are said to have mistaken a shipload of cacao beans for sheep droppings and to have burned the vessel and its precious cargo. On another occasion, the English destroyed more than 100,000 loads of cacao, or 240 million beans, in the Mexican port of Guatulco.[2]

England's first chocolate house was opened in London in 1657 by a Frenchman. The June 6, 1657 issue of the *Public Advertiser* announced, "In Bishopsgate Street, in Queen's Head Alley, at a Frenchman's house, is an excellent West India drink, called Chocolat, to be sold, where you may have it ready at any time; and also unmade, at reasonable prices."

The paper proclaimed chocolate's medicinal qualities, writing that the drink "cures and preserves the body of many diseases."

Reasonable prices, however, were open to interpretation. For despite its widespread acceptance into European society, chocolate's democratization remained many years away. In England, unlike France and other European countries, chocolate was available to whoever could afford the price. But in 1660 the British Parliament raised money for

King Charles II by imposing a seventy-five pence per pound tax on the import of raw cacao beans, thus keeping the processed product out of the reach of the ordinary Briton. If someone was caught smuggling cacao beans, the penalty was one year in prison.

British duties on cacao and gallons of drinking chocolate also served to moderate consumption, which suited the King, who considered chocolate houses hotbeds of sedition. Excessive taxation, however, did not spoil Britain's appetite for chocolate. In 1874, an avant-garde London coffeehouse called At the Coffee Mill and Tobacco Roll began serving chocolate in cakes and rolls in the Spanish tradition.

Despite its popularity, the chocolate drink that consumed Europe in the eighteenth century bears precious little resemblance to the drinking chocolate we enjoy today. The problem was with the cacao bean itself.

To produce a drink, the bean has to be ground into what is commonly known as chocolate liquor. The crude processes to create early European drinking chocolate involved roasting the cacao bean and grinding it into chocolate liquor. The liquor contained 53 percent fat or cacao butter. Once turned into a beverage, the butter would naturally rise to the top in greasy blobs, making the drink unappetizing and sometimes difficult to digest.

The Aztecs crudely tried to solve the problem by adding ground maize to absorb the fat. Europeans either boiled the liquid, skimming the butter from the top, or also used starch-based substances such as rice and barely. The solution, however, was to separate the cacao butter from the solid.

Remarkably, the Spanish were largely silent during this stage of chocolate's evolving history. In the late eighteenth century, chocolate factories were springing up across Europe. Many struggled unsuccessfully to develop a process that would separate, or at least reduce, the amount of cacao butter contained in the chocolate liquor. In 1815, Coenraad Johannes van Houten, a Dutch chemist, began work in his Amsterdam factory on a process that would revolutionize the manufacture of drinking chocolate while paving the way for eating chocolate.

By 1828, van Houten had patented the world's first hydraulic press. The hand-operated device reduced the cacao butter contained in the roasted bean by approximately 25 percent, leaving behind a "cake" that could be pulverized into the powder we now know as cocoa (or cocoa essence, as it was called in van Houten's time).

Van Houten went on to treat the cocoa with alkaline salts (potassium or sodium carbonates) to improve its blending with hot water. This process is known as "Dutching," and it also darkens the colour of the chocolate while producing a milder flavour.

For the first time, cheap chocolate powder could be produced for the masses. Ten years after he had patented the process, van Houten sold the rights to his cocoa press. One of his first customers was J.S. Fry & Sons of Bristol, England.

The full legacy of van Houten's contribution to chocolate making lies not completely in what his press created — cocoa — but what it left behind: a source of pure cacao butter. The melting point of cacao butter is approximately 35°C, which means that it remains solid at room temperature. By returning a portion of the butter to the paste, it would create a soft, smooth form of chocolate that one could eat rather than drink.

J.S. Fry & Sons are largely acknowledged as the first to successfully produce a variety of eating chocolate. By 1847, the firm had perfected a process that mixed cocoa powder with sugar and melted cacao butter to produce a chocolate paste that could be poured into moulds.

The chocolate that came out of those moulds was coarse and gritty, its flavour harsh, but the public did not seem to mind. This was at a time when the English considered most things French to represent the highest standard in both beauty and good taste. Seizing on the mood, Fry's named its first edible chocolate, "Chocolat Délicieux à Manger." Fry's chocolate was first exhibited in 1849 at a trade fair in Birmingham, England, where it became an instant success.

As companies such as rival Cadbury Brothers of Birmingham raced to duplicate Fry's success with even smoother and tastier products, the cost of the once trouble-some cacao butter skyrocketed (today it is one of the world's most expensive edible natural fats).

Less than a quarter of a century after van Houten's cocoa press had made drinking chocolate available to the masses, the inflated price of cacao butter once again created a social divide. The cost of manufacturing eating chocolate priced the product out of the reach of most people. Drinking chocolate, once the exclusive indulgence of the privileged, was now considered common.

Still, refinements to chocolate making continued. Swiss chocolatier Philippe Suchard invented the world's first mélangeur, or mixing machine, in 1826. In 1879, another Swiss chocolatier, Rodolphe Lindt, invented the process of continuously stirring chocolate in its final product stages, creating the first melting chocolate. The process was known as conching.

Conching puts the chocolate through a kneading action and takes its name from the shell-like shape of the containers originally employed. The "conches," as the machines are called, are equipped with heavy rollers that plow back and forth through the chocolate mass for anywhere from a few hours to a few days. Under regulated speeds, these rollers can produce different degrees of agitation and aeration in developing and modifying the chocolate flavours.

In some manufacturing setups, there is an emulsifying operation that either takes the place of conching or else supplements it. A machine works like an eggbeater to break up sugar crystals and other particles in the chocolate mixture to give it a fine, velvety smoothness.

After the emulsifying or conching machines, the mixture goes through a tempering interval — heating, cooling, and reheating — and then at last into moulds to be formed into the shape of the complete product. The moulds take a variety of shapes and sizes, from the popular individual bars available to consumers to the ten-pound blocks used by confectionery manufacturers.

The creation of milk chocolate did not occur until 1867, although the first blending of chocolate liquor with hot milk to create a creamy chocolate drink dates back to 1727. The difficulty in marrying milk with chocolate is easy to understand. Chocolate is 80 percent fat, while milk is 89 percent water. As was the case with cacao butter separating from chocolate drink, fat and water do not mix.

In 1867, Henri Nestlé, a Swiss chemist, discovered a process to make condensed milk through evaporation. David Peter, a Swiss chocolatier, took the process one step further. By adding cocoa powder and sugar to condensed milk and kneading it, Peter created the chocolate crumb essential in the manufacture of today's chocolate bars.

The dry chocolate crumb was mixed with additional cacao butter, chocolate liquor, and other ingredients, then turned into a paste and ground until smooth. Early Nestlé milk chocolate raised the standard of making chocolate in Europe, but it was time-consuming to make and expensive to buy. It took Nestlé close to a week to produce a single batch. Meanwhile, manufacturers elsewhere in Europe tried to work around Nestlé's closely guarded secret with formulas of their own.

Secrecy is as much the lifeblood of the confectionery industry as the veins of cocoa butter and syrup that flow into the making of chocolate and candies.

Where methods of manufacturing are concerned, manufacturers have developed individual variations from the pattern. Each manufacturer seeks to protect his methods by conducting certain operations under an atmosphere of secrecy. Modern technology, in this respect, is reminiscent of the day of the Spanish monopoly.

Today's secrets, unlike those of old, include many small but important details, which centre on key manufacturing operations. Consequently, no chef guards his favourite recipes more zealously than the chocolate manufacturer guards his formulas for blending beans or the time intervals he gives to his conching. Time intervals, temperatures, and proportions of ingredients are three critical factors that no company wants to divulge.

Chocolate viscosity tests are important in the stabilization and control of chocolate coatings.

# Chocolate Arrives in Canada 3

It is well documented that J.S. Fry & Sons marketed the world's first edible chocolate, showcasing its gritty concoction to the delight of those attending a trade fair in Birmingham, England, in 1849. But who invented the world's first mass-produced, mass-marketed, low-cost chocolate bar?

Tagged in North America as the five-cent bar, this particular wrapped tablet of chocolate would become a staple on candy store shelves until (in Canada at least) confectioners first tried to bury the product in 1947 under the burden of a 60 percent price increase. The bar would eventually become the victim of runaway inflation by the 1970s, when manufacturers also abandoned the practice of stamping the price on each candy wrapper before it left the factory.

As for who invented the five-cent chocolate bar, that depends on who is telling the story. The Hershey bar — that quintessential piece of modern day Americana, popularized in no small measure by American GIs in the Second World War — is commonly credited to be the first of what we today consider to be a milk chocolate bar. And with good cause. Still, history points to a Canadian connection.

Milton Hershey, philanthropist, candy enthusiast, and chocolate pioneer, was certainly a visionary. A successful caramel manufacturer from Pennsylvania, Hershey is reported to have realized the enormous potential of chocolate during a visit to the World's Columbian Exposition in Chicago in 1893 (missing the four hundredth anniversary of Christopher Columbus's arrival in America by one year).

While in Chicago, Hershey became fascinated by the operation of German chocolate-making machinery, waiting until closing of the exposition to purchase the equipment. He originally wanted to manufacture a chocolate coating for his caramels.

One year later, Hershey sold his first milk chocolate bar. He continued producing small quantities of the chocolate while focusing on the bigger picture: a process to mass-produce a milk chocolate bar that would be consistent and have a shelf life of weeks, rather than the quick-to-spoil bar he was currently selling.

The stumbling block for Hershey, as it was for all pretenders and refiners of Henri Nestlé's breakthrough, was a recipe that would blend a batch of milk with the other ingredients necessary to manufacture chocolate. At the same time that Hershey was trying to create the "great American chocolate bar," Arthur Ganong, the fourth son and sixth child of Canadian candy pioneer James Ganong, was running the company he inherited from his father in 1888.

By the time Arthur Ganong took the reins, the company his father and uncle founded had grown from a struggling up-market grocery that outsourced the manufacture of its brand-name candy to a bustling candy factory churning out a wide variety of confections.

Like Hershey, the Ganongs had been selling bars of chocolate since before the turn of the century. An 1898 price list of Ganong products includes bars made with coconut and cream fillings.

A Ganong ad, 1893.

In 1910, Arthur and George Ensor, one of Ganong's candymakers, began experimenting with their own brand of milk chocolate using fresh milk from Jersey cows grazing on Arthur's property in St. Stephen, New Brunswick. The two developed a recipe for milk chocolate sprinkled with nuts and shaped into long, narrow pieces.

So pleased were Arthur and George with the finished product that they took the bars to snack on during fishing trips. Ganong began mass-producing and selling their first nickel bar that same year, and continued production until shortly after the breakout of the Second World War.

Wash drawing of the original Ganong candy factory in St. Stephen, New Brunswick.

For their part, Hershey Food neither agrees nor disputes whether Ganong has a legitimate claim. As author David Folster notes in his historical account of the Ganongs, a reporter for Canadian Press wrote that the American company "does not quarrel with the claim that the Ganong family of St. Stephen, N.B., invented the chocolate bar in 1910 — in fact, it is unaware of it."[3]

As recently as September 2000, Maclean's magazine listed the chocolate bar alongside the zipper, frozen food, snow blower, and Fuller Brush as Canadian firsts. At the very least, Arthur and George should be credited with inventing the first chocolate bar mixed with nuts. But even this is in dispute by American writer Ray Broekel, who claims Squirrel Brand of Cambridge, Massachusetts, created the first nut bar in 1906.

Before there was Ganong candy available in New Brunswick, however, there was Moirs in neighbouring Nova Scotia.

In 1815, shortly after arriving in Nova Scotia from Scotland, Benjamin Moir began selling bread and other baked goods to Imperial troops from his modest home in Halifax. The troops were housed in the neighbouring

Citadel, overlooking Halifax harbour. The Citadel had been built by the British sixty-six years earlier as one of four overseas naval stations.

Benjamin's son William C. Moir inherited the bakery in 1845, first changing the name of the business to the Moir & Company Steam Bakery and Flour Mill, and later moving to a five-storey factory on Argyle Street, across from a site that would eventually become Halifax City Hall.

William was anxious that his own "lean stripling" of a son, James, also learned the bakery business. James, who was already described as something of a renegade, went through the motions of learning the skills of a baker, but did not share his father or grandfather's enthusiasm for the trade. Mom-and-pop candymakers like McCormick's Limited in London, Ontario were springing up across Canada, and James struggled to convince his father that there was a future in chocolate and other confectionery.

Despite his father's protestations, James continued to be consumed with the development of sugared almonds and popular candy sticks, often ignoring the day-to-day responsibilities of the family business. Finally, in 1873, a reluctant William Moir relented. "If you're going to fool around with this candy business, you had better take a corner over there and get on with it," he told his son.

Eighteen seventy-three was, indeed, an interesting year for the Canadian confectionery industry. Rather than a year of great hope, which would feed the appetite for such businesses, it was the start of a five-year depression spurred on by a financial panic in New York that September.

It was against this backdrop of collapsing prices, high unemployment, and depressed growth that two brothers opened a general store in St. Stephen, New Brunswick, an industrial town on the banks of the St. Croix River.

The two native New Brunswickers, James Ganong,

Gilbert White Ganong, co-founder of the company.

James Harvey Ganong, co-founder of the company.

who had left Canada and was a salesman for the Thurston & Hall Biscuit Co. of Cambridgeport, Massachusetts, and Gilbert, who taught school outside of St. John, had hoped to attract custom by offering a better range of groceries than was currently available. The enterprise proved to be more difficult than either could have imagined.

There was not much money in St. Stephen during those days, and local residents were suspicious of the strange new upstarts. Compounding the problem was the fact that millworkers who lived in neighbouring communities were either poorly paid or were provided with goods from the company store in exchange for their hard labour.

The pessimism in St. Stephen contrasted sharply with the optimism in Halifax, where James Moir was finally handed the opportunity to trade the flour and yeast of baking for the sugar, molasses, and cocoa of confectionery, full-time. By day he would experiment with different types of chocolate blends in a small corner in the Moirs factory, and by night he would sit on Citadel Hill, not far from where his grandfather first began supplying baked goods to British soldiers, tasting his experiments.

It was during these years that James developed the family XXX formula for what would later become the mainstay of Moirs chocolates.

As Halifax entered the last decade of the nineteenth century, William Moir decided it was time for his son to take over the business. In 1890, seventeen years after James had been given free rein to make candy rather than bake bread, he became president and general manager, immediately increasing the presence of candy in the company's growing product line.

The history of Moirs was part of a pattern in early Canadian candymaking that concentrated the bulk of the new country's confectionery industry in the east. But chocolate did not transport well in the nineteenth century and was in fact expensive to ship. This barrier alone gave rise to small mom-and-pop candymakers, producing small batches of candy suited to local and often neighbourhood tastes.

L.H. Belanger, which began manufacturing candies in Montreal in 1881, produced an elaborate soft toffee called St. Catherine, which has never sold well outside of Quebec despite the one-time popularity of a cheaper version of toffee-based candy chews called Halloween Kisses.

All major candymakers in Canada faced common challenges: importing expensive ingredients such as sugar and cocoa (essential to manufacturing chocolate and candies) and serving a small population narrowly spread out in concentrated pockets along the world's longest border.

Feeding such a population base was difficult enough for confectioners in the east. The challenge was magnified west of the Ontario border. Western-based independents with aspirations to follow the pace set by the Moirs and Ganong families often found they could not gather the traction to break out of local markets.

It is for this reason that the multinational manufacturers based in the east today provide the bulk of confections to satisfy the sweet tooth of western Canadians. There are notable exceptions.

Charles W. Rogers was born in Boston, Massachusetts, in 1854. Rogers was lured out west by the prospect of Klondike gold, but he never made it to the Klondike. He saw greater potential in Victoria selling provisions to the miners.

In 1885, Rogers and his wife, Leah, opened a small greengrocer on Victoria's Government Street, a high-traffic thoroughfare that cut through the heart of the city up to the British Columbia legislature. The shop sold a variety of staple items, fresh fruits and vegetables, and a selection of quality candies imported from San Francisco. Candy was the most popular item on the Rogerses shelves, but delivery was hopelessly erratic, and the high tariffs contained in Prime Minister Sir John A. Macdonald's National Policy of 1878 made it unnecessarily expensive.

Rogers began experimenting with his own candy recipes in a small kitchen located at the back of his store. He would often rise at 4:00 A.M., dressed only in his red underwear, stirring his candy centres as they bubbled in a large copper kettle. Leah, who had previously worked as a printing typesetter with the *Daily Colonist*, looked after the retail trade and administration.

Local inhabitants and visitors to Victoria travelled to Rogers' shop to purchase assortments of chocolate-coated caramels, mint wafers, and chocolate almond brittle. As the candy side of the business grew, fruits and vegetables were getting in the way. Charles and Leah decided to discontinue the grocery side of the business and concentrate on candy.

"A pattern soon developed," wrote *camagazine*. "Charles and Leah would make their chocolates early each day. The store on Government Street would open for a few hours in the afternoon, and, once the last chocolate was sold, the doors would close."

On occasion, Charles and Leah were forced to ration boxes of their chocolates to one per customer.

In 1888, Rogers introduced his most unique and popular creation, cream centres covered with dark chocolate in a range of flavours, including vanilla, peppermint, chocolate nut, and strawberry.

It is interesting to note that a few years later, Frank Mars, an amateur candymaker, penny candy salesman, and father of Forrest Mars, founder of the multinational confectionery and food giant that bears his family name, was struggling to set up his own candy company in neighbouring Seattle.

It is not known whether Mars senior ever bit into a Rogers Victoria Cream, but the man who liked to experiment with his mother's candy recipes began selling Victorian Butter Creams through the Woolworth five-and-ten store chain in the 1920s.

"Butter Creams were fairly common," explains Jim Ralph, president of Rogers' Chocolates. And there is a difference between the Butter Cream and Rogers' Victoria Creams. "But it's interesting that [Mars] would call his chocolates Victorian Butter Creams," Ralph adds.

The origin of the Victoria Cream recipe remains a mystery. Most of Rogers' work was trial and error, often conducted while hunched over a cauldron of chocolate. Victoria Creams were also the most expensive candies in the shop.

Rogers, the man who began making his own candy to spare the expense of importing confections from San Francisco, was later forced to admonish any young consumer fortunate enough to have ten cents to spend, but naive enough to think he could purchase a selection of Victoria Creams. "Ten cents buys you one chocolate," he'd be told curtly.

Charles Rogers was notorious for his lack of patience with those who came into his shop. In addition to keeping odd hours — ignoring the lines outside the shop and only opening when he was ready — Rogers was often surly and rarely exchanged niceties or indulged in idle chatter.

Above all, Rogers appeared to cherish his privacy. This was confirmed in a historical retrospective published by the *Victoria Times Colonist* in 1951. Charles Rogers, the article reported, "seems to have succeeded fairly well in pulling a blind down around himself. Even when he married, in 1885, an 'estimable young lady for many years a resident of Victoria', the local papers were discreetly non-committed. For he was, at the time, according to the reports, a 'worthy and energetic young man having established himself in a lucrative business.'"[4]

But the couple worked hard. On the coldest winter nights they would often stay in their shop to sleep only to get up before the sun to start working again. They also took few holiday trips, preferring instead to check into the St. Joseph's hospital for a week whenever they felt they needed a respite.

In the 1890s, Frederick Barnes Wood moved from Nova Scotia to the British territory of Newfoundland. Upon arrival in St. John's, Wood opened a fruit, confectionery, and flower shop. He too wanted to secure a steady supply of quality goods for his store and began manufacturing his own line of candies, alongside jellies, syrups, and marmalades.

In the early twentieth century Wood decided to transfer his shop to a magnificent new building on St. John's fashionable Water Street. *The Evening Telegram* wrote about the new shop on January 11, 1902. "Woods new candy store is all but complete. A credit to all concerned."

Certainly it was something that few residents of St. John's had seen before: a candy shop, bakery, and soda fountain on the ground floor, beneath an elegant restaurant complete with starched white table linen and equally starched serving staff. The candy store and restaurant quickly became one of the most patronized locations in St. John's.

The Water Street location would have a short run. Wood closed the shop in 1917 to concentrate exclusively on a second restaurant. In 1923, he retired completely, selling his business interests to W.R. Goodie, a local businessman who would transform Wood's confectionery and soda pop interests into Purity Factories Ltd., the province's largest confectioner and home to some of Newfoundland's traditional favourites.

It was also during the nineteenth century that the story of what would become Canada's largest chocolate company began. In the early 1800s, John Nilson, a weaver by trade, and his wife, Agnes, left the textile town of Paisley, Scotland, to seek new opportunities for themselves and their four children in the largely unsettled colony of Upper Canada.

With their ocean passage sponsored by the British government and a small parcel of rugged, untended land awaiting them on the other side, the Nilsons endured a rough and often violent seven-week voyage, docking in Montreal, Lower Canada, on June 19, 1821.

The journey across land, river, and lake from Montreal to Almonte, Upper Canada, was not without its own hardships and damp discomforts. The Nilsons had cast off the impoverished veils of a weaver's family to assume the role of impoverished pioneer farmers in a land as strange to them as the home they had left behind was familiar. Despite the hardships, John harboured no regrets.

In a personal letter reprinted on the editorial pages of the *Almonte Gazette*, the grandfather of William Neilson wrote, "I have no cause to regret the step that I took when I left Paisley. The weaving had been poor employment. You might exert yourself to the utmost, but poverty would stare you in the face. But Canada is a place where a man can exert himself to good purpose."

Portions of the family's past remain clouded. It is not known when or why the Nilsons abandoned the Scandinavian spelling of the family name for the traditionally Scottish "Neilson." Nor is there a lot of detail about John Jr., eldest son of John and Agnes, and father of William Neilson.

William Neilson had inherited more of his Scottish grandfather's sense of independence than his own father's love of the land. Born in Almonte, Canada West (the territorial successor to Upper Canada) on March 16, 1844, the eldest son of John and Mary Neilson had grown restless and dissatisfied with conditions in the British colony. In 1865, at age twenty-one, William Neilson left the small family farm to see out a new life in Rochester, New York.

He left the United States in 1867, but not before meeting the woman he would one day marry. Mary Eva Kaiser was the daughter of a prominent Rochester farming family. A resourceful and determined woman, the future Mrs. Neilson is credited with finding grist for the fledgling Neilson mill during the lean years when money was tight or when her husband was forced to hunt for work away from home.

Neilson did not return to Almonte. His ambitions had outgrown his hometown and the family farm. Instead, he chose to relocate in the capital city of the new province called Ontario, in the new country called Canada.

While walking along the bustling dirt road that was Yonge Street in the heart of Toronto's commercial district, Neilson was drawn to a small retail store advertising homemade ice cream. The selling of ice cream in those days was done without packaging. There were no cones or wax-treated cartons. The proprietor would cut slabs of the frozen treat from large tubs and sell it by weight for home use.

Neilson's interest was not with the product or the way it was marketed, but with the machinery. The churning machine that turned dairy liquid and flavouring into bricks of iced cream fascinated him. This blending of machine and dairy product would allow Neilson to take his place alongside Timothy Eaton, Vincent Massey, George Weston, and Joseph Atkinson of the *Toronto Star* as an early Canadian entrepreneur who would carve his name into Toronto's corporate landscape.

But it was Brockville, Ontario, 340 kilometres east of Toronto, that marked a turning point in William Neilson's life. Secure with the wages of a millwright, Neilson briefly return to Rochester to propose to his American sweetheart, Mary Eva Kaiser. They were married and returned to Brockville, where they had five children. But the security of Neilson's trade would not last.

The restlessness that had driven William from the farm eventually pushed him away from the nuts and bolts of machinery to the wooden floors and glass counters of the retail trade. He opened General Fancy Goods, a short-lived dry goods store that suffered from a depressed economy and the proprietor's willingness to extend credit to customers caught in the squeeze.

Frustrated by his lacklustre entry into Brockville's sluggish retail trade, William Neilson considered selling the store and moving the family to Chicago. The store was sold and the family did move, but part of the purchase price included a property in Toronto.

Disappointed but not discouraged by his first attempt at merchandising, William Neilson rented a new store, put on a grocer's apron, and tried again. Again the state of the economy and the generosity of the novice grocer dampened the potential of the business. It was a bitter experience. In Brockville, slow-paying customers eventually settled their debts. In Toronto, many of Neilson's customers felt no similar compulsion. By the summer of 1891, his capital was exhausted and his income had dried up. He returned to the United States to work on his brother Jessie's North Dakota farm for four dollars a day.

Although Neilson sent his wages back to Toronto, his wife, Mary, found that it was not sufficient to support their five children. In later years, Morden Neilson would recall the extreme poverty of his youth and the way he had to wriggle into a pair of his mother's shoes when he did not have his own to wear.

More resourceful than frugal, Mary Neilson drew from the experience of her youth on the Kaiser farm in Rochester. She rented a house on four acres of land on Toronto's Lynd Avenue and began growing her own fruits and vegetables to put food on the table, and she had enough left over to sell to the neighbours.

By the time Neilson returned to Toronto, Mary had built up a local customer base for one of her most popular items, homemade mincemeat. The family was still in debt, but relief was around the corner. With a few milking cows and a steady demand for mincemeat, the Neilsons went into business for themselves. They were lean years. William sold the mincemeat to local retailers while Morden — often dressed in his mother's side-button shoes and his father's worn trousers cut off at the knees — went from door to door with pails of milk on his way to school.

In later years, a stop at the Neilson booth in the Food Building would be one of the highlights of a trip to Toronto's annual Canadian National Exhibition. But in the late 1800s, William Neilson could not scrape together the price of an admission ticket for Morden to attend the annual fair. He suggested that his son try to collect the amount from delinquent customers. Morden was not successful.

The first block of Neilson ice cream was sold on May 24, 1893. Months earlier, William Neilson had bought three worn-out, hand-cranked ice cream freezers on four months' extended credit from an acquaintance who had failed in his own attempt to produce and sell the frozen daily treat.

The two-gallon freezers were moved to a barn in the backyard of the Lynd Avenue property, where William, after making repairs, taught members of the family how to operate them. Morden was charged with the manual work of preparing and cranking the mix.

"We had to break the ice for those early tub freezers," he told a businessman's luncheon twenty years later. "But it was the freezers that broke our hearts. All that hand-crank-ing. Besides, father believed that the speed of the freezer would be gradually increased until the climax was reached in a frenzy of speed. You can imagine the demands this made on the strength of those of us who did the cranking."

Morden cranked out ten to twenty two-gallon batches of ice cream a day during the first summer of their opera-tion. A total of 3,750 gallons of ice cream were sold that summer. The more than $3,000 made was the first real cash the family had seen in years.

This was very much a family business. William sold mincemeat, milk, and ice cream door-to-door and from grocery store to grocery store. Morden churned ice cream and delivered pails of milk. In the winter months, another son, Charles, travelled to Grenadier Pond in Toronto's High Park to help carve out large hunks of ice. The ice would be loaded onto horse-drawn wagons, transported to the plant, and stored in sawdust for use in the summer.

*courtesy of National Archives of Canada*

The Moirs selection

At the same time that Neilson's horses were heav-ing blocks of ice through the streets of Toronto, horse-drawn wagons were fanning out across Halifax delivering Moirs goods to local retail-ers. By the early 1900s, the Moirs product line included more than six hundred vari-eties of bread, cake, biscuits, and candies. Many products were placed on trains to feed a growing Canadian appetite.

By 1904, the Neilson family operation had outgrown the Lynd Avenue home where the ice cream was still being cranked by hand.

Confident with the growth of the business, William Neilson purchased property on Gladstone Avenue in Toronto's West End. Within two years of transferring the business from Lynd to Gladstone, the success of ice cream had nudged milk off the Neilson product list.

Some customers viewed the sale of two grades of milk with suspicion. One woman told Morden that she expect-ed the milk quality to be lower now that their ice cream was so successful. Morden was deeply disturbed by this and con-vinced his father to abandon the milk business and concen-trate on ice cream.

But ice cream was a seasonal product. In the early 1900s, more ice cream was sold during the summer months than throughout the other three seasons combined. William Neilson's challenge was to stretch the sales peak beyond the summer and to provide year-round jobs for the company's employees. The answer lay in a distant cousin of ice cream: chocolate.

In 1906, Neilson began producing bulk and boxed chocolate in the Gladstone plant as seasonal filler. But Neilson's chocolate became a year-round favourite, and the idea of juggling employees between the peaks and valleys of chocolate and ice cream production eventually turned out to be unworkable.

"We could not afford to dispense with skilled candy workers in the winter to give employment to ice cream employees," Morden explained in a 1925 interview. "So the two branches of the business were operated quite independently so far as the interchange of labour was concerned."

The most valued ice cream employees were employed during the winter months painting and repairing machinery.

Mincemeat — once the staple of Neilson's door-to-door business — also became a casualty of chocolate pro-duction. Mary's homemade specialty was discontinued in 1907.

Delivering Neilson's chocolate over the years:

by horse and wagon in 1927;

moving up speed with a truck in 1940;

and a VW van in 1960.

At the same time Mary Neilson was hanging up her apron, Richard Cormon Purdy was jumping into the candy business on Canada's West Coast. Today, Purdy's Chocolates is the largest manufacturing retailer of chocolates in British Columbia, and second only to Laura Secord in Canada. Still, very little is known about Richard Purdy himself, even inside the company that bears his name.

"We've never really known much about him. It was only when we registered the name nationwide that we found out what his middle initial stood for," Neil Hastie, then vice-president of retail and marketing, told *Vancouver Magazine* in 1992.

What is known is that Purdy, who first began making chocolates in his home around the turn of the century, was something of a showman who liked to combine the sale of his chocolate creations with a flair for the extravagant. In the early 1920s, Purdy moved out of his first candy store on downtown Vancouver's Robson Street to a more spectacular location on nearby Granville.

The store, which included a candy kitchen in the basement, featured a soda fountain and second floor balcony that encircled the interior. Purdy operated the balcony as the Devon Café. A private switchboard was installed so customers to the Devon Café could call down to the soda fountain using the telephones located on each table. Orders were delivered to the table, with each ice cream sundae topped off with a rich Purdy's chocolate cream.

The chocolate creams were so popular that many customers could not resist purchasing a box from the sales floor below. But while Richard Purdy was a skilled chocolatier and innovative retailer, neither his chocolate creations nor his customers at the Devon Café could support his business.

Purdy's went bankrupt in the 1920s and was purchased by a local businessman, Hugh Forrester, in 1925.

Purdy's logos from 1920 to 1998:

**Things that change** — OUR COMPANY LOGO

1920's

1930's

1950's

1960's

1970's

1980's

1990's

1997

1998

# The History of Sugar Candy

*"They're always eating candy in Shelbyville. They can't get enough of the sweet taste…"*

Milhouse

*The Simpsons* episode 2F21, "Lemon of Troy"

On May 1, 1851, London, England, played host to the world with an Exposition that Queen Victoria's husband, Albert, had orchestrated as an exhibition of nations. Visitors to the exposition (including those from the Canadas) would have been treated to a dazzling display of Europe's finest confectioneries: fancy caramels and smooth chocolate fondant from England, bonbons from France, flavoured lozenges and elaborately decorated hard candies from Germany, and sugarplums from Holland.

At the same time that attendees to the Exposition were marvelling over the art of candymaking, those same European influences were building a candy industry in North America, most notably in Chicago.

Canada has nothing equivalent to Chicago as a candy centre, with its concentration of historic names such as Wrigley, Tootsie Roll Industries, and Archibald (owner of Laura Secord since June 1999).

By 1854, Chicago was reported to have had ten breweries, nine vinegar makers, four pickle warehouses, and no fewer than forty-six confectioners. Today, the Windy City produces one-third of America's candy and is home to much of the retro candy that Canadian baby boomers and their children flock to the reincarnated candy store to purchase.

But Chicago's candy industry grew up much the same way as Canada's did, in the cramped home kitchens of mom-and-pop entrepreneurs. These typically produced enough bite-sized morsels to sell out in a single day before returning to the pans and kettles to make more.

Simply dissolving sugar in water, after all, makes candy. The different heating levels will determine the type of candy. A hot temperature makes hard candy, medium heat will make soft candy, and cool temperatures will produce chewy candy. A skilled sugar boiler often gauged the temperature and texture of the sugar with his finger.

Unlike chocolate, however, the history of candymaking is sometimes as clear as fudge. Take the name, for instance. Did it originate from the ancient Persian word "kand," describing a sweet popular in 325 B.C., or from the Arabic word "qand," meaning sugar?

Certainly sugar is to candymaking what van Houten's press was to the chocolate revolution. But the original manufacture of sweets predates the cultivation of sugarcane by the Arabs in fifth century A.D.

The first gatherer of something sweet was the caveman, who would eat honey straight from the beehive. Honey would remain the essential ingredient in candymaking for centuries to come.

In ancient times, the Egyptians, Arabs, and Chinese would candy fruits and nuts by rolling the ingredients in a mixture of flour and honey. These concoctions were often shaped and baked in furnaces. The honey-based candy was flavoured and thickened by sap flowing from the root of the althe officinalis, or marsh-mallow plant, (also common in the salt marshes of the eastern United States).

The sweet commonly known as Turkish Delight is said to have been available since biblical times. A more modern version, considered to be the origin of the popular jelly-bean, can be traced back to the late 1700s.

Haci Bekir, a confectioner to the Ottoman court, is said to have developed a confection that sultans would eat to wash away the bitter taste of Turkish coffee. The sweet jelly was originally called *rahat ul hulkum* meaning "contentment for the throat" in Arabic. This was shortened to lokum, and later dubbed Turkish Delight by a nineteenth-century English traveller who returned home with the sweet.

Like chocolate, early candy was embraced for more than its taste. According to Whittaker, candy was routinely used "for medication, meditation, resuscitation, as dummies, bribes [and] tokens of love. Confectionery had an all-embracing agenda."[5]

Early Greek and Roman physicians would soften the taste of bitter medicine by rubbing sweetener around the rims of the cups containing the dosage. It was a practice later extended to English chemists, who would sugar-coat pills.

One of the earliest candies to come out of the first millennium was the lozenge, produced by Arabians using powdered sugar, gum Arabic, and gum tragacanth.

In around 1470 the Venetians learned that a fine-grain sugar would result from successive boilings of the cane juice. Sugar became more available throughout Italy and then spread across Europe. The high cost of sugar, however, meant that the commodity was, once again, only available to the wealthy. One of the most ostentatious examples of how sugar could be used at the time occurred during a visit to Venice by Henry III of France. A party was held in the King's honour featuring plates and linen produced from spun sugar.

At last candy was on its way, but equipment was lacking for production in quantity, and the sugar refining processes were expensive. Only the rich could afford refined sugar, and not even all of them had been fortunate enough to taste candy.

Technology would have to reduce both the cost of refining the raw materials (such as sugar cane) and the cost of mass-producing quantities of candy. French innovation not only broadened the range of candies, with creations such as pralines and nougat, but also contributed to time-tested methods of manufacturing. One of the best-known inventions from seventeenth-century France led to the process known as panning.

Panning literally builds a candy by tossing pieces into a revolving pan and adding coating ingredients such as syrup, flavourings, colourings, and other ingredients (including chocolate). On evaporation, these layers form a dry shell around the original candy.

courtesy of Ganong Bros., Ltd.

The starch "mogul" for making centres for chocolates and jelly beans, as well as making jellies, jujubes, and marshmallows, 1940: the "heart" of the company.

The French began by rocking almonds in a bowl filled with sugar and syrup until the pieces were coated with a similar candied shell. Panning has opened the door to many modern day favourites including M&Ms, Red Hots, and that indirect descendant of Turkish Delight, the jelly bean.

Shiny confectionery products can be divided into three categories: chocolate, hard-panned, and soft-panned products. Each type requires its own method of manufacture and shine development. The panning process coats the candy, and the buffing action during the pan's rotation produces the gloss. The key is to first develop the gloss and then to maintain it over the storage life of the candy.

Boiled sugar candies were enjoyed in the seventeenth century in England. Some of the country's earliest confectioners were not particularly discriminating with respect to ingredients. Many would use chorium, copper, mercury, and arsenic extract for colouring. The practice was ended in 1850 when an article in *The Lancet* declared it dangerous.

It is likely that English boiled sweets were among the first candies to arrive in North America, through immigration and Britain's trade with her colonies.

As in the United States, Canada developed a thriving regional penny candy industry, with small family-owned operations filling glass jars at the corner shop with multi-coloured sugar treats.

With its array of intricate recipes and temperamental acceptance of seasons and climate, candymaking was anything but child's play. The same cannot be said for the market. It was the eyes of a child that would widen at the display of glass candy jars crammed with coloured varieties of candy sticks, jelly beans, lemon drops, and mints.

With his brother James often out of town selling biscuits and crackers for Thurston, Hall & Co., it was left to Gilbert Ganong to boost sales in the foundering St. Stephen grocery. He decided that the future was not in general groceries, which could be purchased from more established merchants, but in selling less available specialty items such as fresh oysters, fine cakes, and candy.

Candy was still in its infancy in North America and accounted for no more than $3 million in annual sales, with Canada's small and diverse population responsible for a wafer-thin share of the total.

Ganong's first candies came from a supplier in St. John. Not satisfied by the quality, Gilbert began importing sweets from the United States. The high tariff on imports made Ganong's candies more expensive than locally produced pieces such as those manufactured and sold by Charles M. Holt.

The Ganongs approached Holt to manufacture candies for their store, but he refused. Instead he enlarged his own store, expanding the range of specialty items and cutting the cost of his candies.

The favourite among Canadian children of the time was the candy stick. And so it was that the candy stick became the battlefield where the price war between Charles Holt and the Ganongs erupted. Holt fired first. The candymaker cut the wholesale price of his candy sticks from twenty cents a pound to eighteen cents. He later dropped the price another two cents. On both occasions, the brothers matched the cost, and once again approached Holt about the possibility of buying his candy in bulk.

On this occasion, the candymaker was willing to supply the Ganongs' store, but at a price no less than what he would charge an infrequent customer. Instead, James and Gilbert went across the St. Croix River to Calais, Maine. There they found a candymaker that would manufacture stick candy using sugar supplied by the Ganongs. The candy would also be sold in Calais under the Ganong name.

In 1874, Holt, whose expanded store was struggling, asked the Ganongs if they would be interested in buying his wholesale business and contracting out his well-known skills as a baker and candymaker. At this time, however, James and Gilbert were experiencing cash problems of their own.

Trade at the Ganongs' St. Stephen store, which had expanded during the peak of the aggressive price war, had dropped. A second store fared even worse. This shop had been opened on the St. Stephen side of the toll bridge linking the town with Calais. The plan was to attract people crossing either side of the bridge. But most pedestrians were out of work and did not have money to spend on luxury items such as cake and candy.

The warehouse the brothers rented on the American side to store inventory sold to American merchants proved to be another financial headache. The facility was a regular target for employees stuffing their pockets with Ganong nuts and candies.

In 1875, Charles Holt died suddenly. The Ganongs convinced his widow to install their Calais candymaker in the family bakery. The story of Canada's largest independent confectioner would begin in earnest.

The late nineteenth century was an exciting time to be in the confectionery industry. The depression was over, and consumerism was taking hold. Henry Morgan, a Montreal retailer, had already introduced the department store concept to Canada. Others would follow, including The Hudson Bay Company in Winnipeg (1881) and Woodwards in Vancouver (1892). Each of these stores would open candy departments.

The greatest innovator was Timothy Eaton, who, in 1884, introduced consumers to the wonders of the mail order catalogue. Now Eaton's quality merchandise, including candy, was available through a mail order system that covered Canada from sea to sea (Charles and Leah Rogers would open their own mail order system at the turn of the century).

Sixty years later, in 1940, candy is still a part of Eaton's Winnipeg store.

In the mid nineteenth century, Gilbert Ganong hired Chris Laubman, a young German immigrant who claimed to have come from a long line of skilled German candymakers. The family specialized in the lozenge, a popular Canadian confection available in various flavours, including mint, and often used as a cough suppressant.

The original lozenge machine, 1942. This machine is still operational, and, at over one hundred years old, it is perhaps the oldest working candy machine in the world.

Manufacturers liked the lozenge because it was one of the few candies that did not need to be cooked, and it was impervious to either heat or humidity. Not only did this resistance give the lozenge a longer shelf life, it also made the candy easier to transport.

In 1889, Gilbert installed a European lozenge machine capable of producing thousands of lozenges every day, including a wafer-thin variety not previously available in Canada. The machine worked so well that the company installed a second.

Chris Laubman would become one of three legendary candymakers who would help Ganong to produce innovations such as stick candy with an image or a message (like Merry Christmas) that would run through the length of the confectionery.

Another popular Ganong candy was the All-Day Sucker. The origin of the lollipop, or hard-boiled candy on a stick, remains a mystery. The Racine Confectioners Machinery Company of Racine Wisconsin claims to have developed the first machine to automate the process of lollipop manufacturing in 1908. Samuel Born, a Russian immigrant living in San Francisco at the turn of the century, is said to have invented a machine to put hard candy on a stick in 1916.

Both inventions lag behind the day that the Ganongs introduced hard candy on a stick to Canada in 1895. The wooden sticks were similar to what the neighbourhood butcher used to fasten the meat. A stick was pressed into a warm piece of candy and left behind as the candy hardened.

Ganong produced its All-Day Suckers in several flavours, including strawberry, lemon, peppermint, licorice, and orange. Rival companies across Canada would soon duplicate the simple invention, and by the end of the century, All-Day Suckers had surpassed candy sticks as Canada's favourite penny candy.

A notice of Doerr's opening in Berlin, in both English and German.

But Gilbert and James Ganong were not the only grocers who began making candy to stock store shelves. In 1892, Charles H.

Doerr, a German immigrant living in Berlin, Ontario (now Kitchener), and Ted Egan, a baker from neighbouring Guelph, agreed to open a bakery.

The original plan was to manufacture biscuits and sell them in Doerr's store, which he had opened some years earlier on the northern edge of the city near tracks belonging to the Grand Trunk Railway.

Berlin was a thriving industrial centre in 1892. German and English immigrants secured jobs in the community's meat packing, leather, and furniture industries. The city was also a gateway for settlers travelling west to the Prairies. Berliners and transients relied on local merchants to supply them with provisions such as clothing and food.

Doerr and Egan were enjoying such a healthy trade in biscuits and recently introduced candies that the store stopped carrying groceries. Eventually the factory would also eclipse the store, although there are indications that by this point, Egan had left the business.

In the early days, Doerr did everything but bake the product. Because there were no supermarket chains or centralized buying groups, biscuits and candies were sold in bulk to individual neighbourhood stores. Several times a year, Doerr would hook horse to carriage and begin a town-by-town sales trip. Customers sampled his products and placed their orders, which were filled and shipped out by train.

The company's candy line included a broad range of handmade products. Popular hard candies and gumdrops were supplemented by specialties such as chocolate-coated marshmallow Easter eggs and Christmas favourites such as cut rock candy and colourful satin mix.

Soon major national retail chains, such as Woolworth and Kresge, were distributing Doerr products across the country.

Hard candy department at Dare in 1913.

Dare delivery horse and carriage.

# Bubble Gum 5

Bubble gum represents something of a detour in the story of candy. A hybrid of chewing gum and pan candy that, unlike suckers and candy sticks, does not fit comfortably into the sugar category, bubble gum is also an American invention that has evolved into something of a Canadian success story.

Canada is one of the largest exporters of multicoloured gumballs, and a Canadian company owns the syrupy recipes, brands, trademark oval, and comic strip characters of the Coca Cola of all bubble gum: Dubble Bubble.

The chewing of gum — or at least the chewing of tree resin — can be traced back to prehistoric times. The first written record of gum chewing appears in Greece in the first century AD. The Mayans chewed a gooey substance from the sapodilla tree (the civilization's main source of fruit) that they called chicle. Mayans chewed chicle after meals to help with their digestion, and during the day to quench their thirst.

Christopher Columbus witnessed natives in Santo Domingo (now the Dominican Republic) chewing mastic gum in 1492. He wrote about the custom, but there is no evidence to suggest that he was any more enthusiastic about gum than he was about chocolate twenty years later.

Hernán Cortés is reported to have remarked on the Aztecs having the whitest teeth he had ever seen, crediting this early dental hygiene to the chewing of chicle.

Unlike chocolate and candy, however, North Americans outside of Mexico did not wait for gum to come to them. Native Americans were chewing tangy spruce resin before the arrival of the Pilgrims in the early 1600s. The first commercial chewing gum was manufactured in 1848 in Maine.

In 1869, Thomas Adams, a Staten Island photographer and inventor, purchased a ton of chicle from Antonio Lopez de Santa Anna, the deposed and exiled former president of Mexico. As was the custom, Santa Anna used chicle for chewing. Adams wanted to use the hardened sap to manufacture rubber. When this failed, Adams made batches of chewing gum on the top of his stove, testing the popularity of gum at his local druggist.

Two years later, Adams patented a gum-making machine that kneaded the chicle and flattened it into long, thin wafers that merchants would dispense to customers by breaking pieces from a rolled gum strip.

Adams continued to experiment. He added shredded licorice to the chicle to produce the legendary Black Jack chewing gum. He used the panning method to produce Tutti-Frutti, a selection of candy-coated gumballs available in several colours and flavours.

Tutti-Frutti was the first gum available through a coin-fed vending machine. The vending machine was first introduced in London, England, in the early 1800s to dispense postcards. Adams's refined gumball machines were installed on platforms along New York City's elevated railway in 1888.

Adams's gumballs were popular. But the colourful candied pieces weren't bubble gum. At the turn of the century, chewing gum — including William Wrigley Jr.'s highly successful Spearmint gum — did not have the strength to hold a balloon shape as the bubble got larger, stretching the gum thinner. Nor did gum have the necessary elasticity to return to its original shape within a split second of the bubble bursting.

Frank H. Fleer, a salesman for a family company manufacturing candy flavouring, understood the potential of chewing gum. Adams and Wrigley were already successful producers. Not only did North Americans love the stuff, their doctors would often recommend gum to relax facial muscles.

Fleer wanted to manufacture gum that was fun. The thickness of spruce and the sticky properties of chicle, however, limited the opportunity for a "fun" chew in the early 1900s. That did not prevent Fleer from manufacturing different flavours of chewing gum while he experimented to produce a synthetic gum base that could be blown into bubbles.

His first attempt to market bubble gum in 1906 failed miserably. Blibber-Blubber had the surface strength to hold a bubble, but it lacked the elasticity needed to snap back.

Instead, Fleer's gum would stick to the blower's face and have to be cleaned off using turpentine.

By 1910, the Philadelphia-based Fleer Chewing Gum Company had introduced its own version of candy-coated gum called Chiclets (which would later be produced by Adams). But a formula for gum that was truly fun would consume and elude the company's founder for the rest of his life.

Fun would not arrive until August 1928, when Walter E. Diemer, a twenty-three-year-old accountant perhaps more interested in gum recipes than financial statements, stumbled upon the formula for the perfect bubble gum. Diemer, who was employed by Fleer, shared the company's desire to realize Frank Fleer's vision.

For a year, Diemer would work on Fleer's accounts by day and experiment with gum recipes at his Philadelphia home by night. By trial and error the young accountant created a substance that was less sticky than regular chewing gum but more resilient when stretched. Diemer produced five pounds of the glop and amazed his employers and colleagues by the ease with which he could blow bubbles and peel the gum off his face once the bubble popped.

Unfortunately, the first batch of bubble gum had a very short shelf life. Within twenty-four hours, the first five-pound batch lost whatever chemistry had allowed it to be blown. After another four months Diemer improved his recipe, this time manufacturing three hundred pounds of bubble gum in a company mixer just before Christmas. The gum was a bright pink, because that was the only bottle of colouring on hand at the time.

Fleer christened the product Dubble Bubble and began selling individual pieces in a small candy store in Philadelphia the day after Christmas, 1928. Each piece was wrapped using second-hand taffy-wrapping machines that Diemer had located in Atlantic City.

By the time the stock market bubble burst in 1929, Dubble Bubble was outselling Tootsie Roll as America's favourite piece of penny candy. Fleer would not own the bubble gum market for very long. Diemer had not patented the recipe, opening the gates for flood of imitators (although Bazooka bubble gum did not come onto the market until after World War II).

Perhaps to excite young consumers to buy more, Fleer inserted a black-and-white comic into each piece of gum in 1930. The first comics featured the Dubble Bubble twins, Dub and Bub. Both characters were replaced by Pud, the bubble gum's present-day cartoon mascot, in 1950. In 1968, the one thousandth Dubble Bubble comic strip was printed, and by 1981, Fleer was selling over one million pieces of Pud's favourite chew in over fifty countries around the world.

Canada's connection with Dubble Bubble doesn't begin until 1996, although it can be traced to 1986, when Concord Confections began manufacturing bubble gum and other candy products in Concord, Ontario.

The Fleer Corporation was purchased in 1992 by the acquisition-hungry Marvel Entertainment Group, publisher of such comic book stalwarts as Spiderman, the Incredible Hulk, and X-Men. By this time, Fleer was known as much for its trading cards as its bubble gum.

The company had produced its first "famous pictures" series in 1923, featuring 120 baseball heroes, including Babe Ruth. A set of trading cards highlighting cops and robbers appeared in 1935. But the company would not get serious about sports trading cards until 1959, nine years after rival Topps.

For two years, Marvel rode a market bubble inflated by a new generation of amateur collectors anxious to get their hands on old comic books (many bundled up in the basements belonging to the parents of baby boomers) and first year rookie cards. By 1993, retailers were selling comics and trading cards by the case to gullible young consumers who believed they were buying items worth collecting.[6]

In 1994, Fleer accounted for approximately 50 percent of Marvel's revenue. The company expanded its trading card business by purchasing Skybox in 1995. By then, the bubble had already popped. As player strikes infiltrated professional sports, the collectors lost interest in trading cards promoting athletes.

Comic books weren't faring any better as speculators realized that over-supply, particularly for sought-after special editions, was dampening investment value. Marvel flooding the market with poorly illustrated comics during the height of the craze did not help.

Caught in a market revolt, combating a hostile takeover, and struggling to rescue its ailing comic book and trading card businesses, Marvel neglected its bubble gum business. Pud and the Dubble Bubble brand stumbled.

By then, ten-year-old Concord Confections was manufacturing tens of millions of gumballs a day, including the original extra sour gumball. The company was exporting Tongue Splashers, Kid Gumball, and Bubble Blox to more than fifty-two countries in six continents.

The company approached Marvel about purchasing the Dubble Bubble brand. Marvel filed for Chapter 11 bankruptcy protection shortly after. In 1998, Concord made headlines by purchasing Dubble Bubble for US$13 million and assuming approximately US$6 million in debt — considerably less than the US$286 million Marvel had paid for Fleer in 1992 (although Marvel kept the trading card side and eventually spun the enterprise off as Fleer/Skybox).

The *Globe and Mail* described the takeover as "the bubble gum equivalent of Seagram Co. Ltd.'s take-over of PolyGram NV." Paul Cherrie, then managing director of the privately owned Concord, was more focused. "This is the Jell-O or Kool-Aid of the bubble gum industry. "

In addition to Dubble Bubble's secret formula, Pud, and its distinctive crown and blue oval logo, Concord took over Fleer's plants in Mississippi, Germany, and Spain. In 1999, Concord introduced a first in the American bubble gum's seventy-one-year history by marketing coloured gumballs under the Dubble Bubble name.

On her website, *An American's Guide to Canada*, Emily Way gives Thrills pride of place alongside Canadian Tire money and wearing a poppy on Remembrance Day. "A purple gum that looks like Chiclets. I've never tried it — I have some sitting in the cupboard downstairs, but I loathe gum — but everyone says, 'tastes like soap!' whenever it's mentioned."

# An Industry Takes Hold (1900-1920)

*"What use are cartridges in battle? I always carry chocolate instead."*

George Bernard Shaw

In the fourteen years between the arrival of the twentieth century and the outbreak of the Great War, confectionery was becoming a crowded and competitive industry in Canada. As a barometer, the import of cocoa had increased 70 percent between 1900 and 1904. Ganong, Moirs, William Neilson, Willa'rds, and Rogers' had built

manufacturing facilities in different parts of the country, while several foreign candymakers, like Walter Lowney, were assessing the market.

The candy industry was just as frantic as kids reached into their pockets and pulled out coins to purchase their favourite penny candies. There was a lot to choose from. Robertson Brothers Ltd. of Toronto was turning out approximately 250 different candy pieces. Ganong only had 150 pieces, but would introduce three new candies every month while removing three less popular sellers from the store shelves.

Packing Ganong coconut bonbons in wooden tubs, 1910.

*courtesy of Ganong Bros., Ltd.*

Amidst this bustle came Canada's most historically significant brand of chocolates. In 1913, Frank O'Connor opened a small candy store on the corner of Toronto's Yonge and Elm Streets. The exterior was painted white with black trim, its windows accented with muslin polka dot curtains. "It will look homey," O'Connor said, "and the candies will seem homey." Inside, the shelves were stocked with chocolates and other confections he made upstairs in his apartment.

The first Laura Secord shop, located at Yonge and Elm streets in Toronto, 1913.

Wishing to capitalize on Canadian patriotism, O'Connor decided to name his candy after Laura Secord, the Massachusetts-born expatriate who became a Canadian heroine by spying on American troops during the War of 1812.

In the spring of 1813, the Americans already occupied the Canadian side of the Niagara River. Laura, the wife of a sergeant seriously injured in October 1812, after the Americans had attacked Queenston Heights, learned of an invasion planned for Beaver Dams. Laura Secord walked for eighteen hours through swamp, bush, and farmland to warn Lieutenant Fitzgibbon of the impending attack. The British were able to surprise the Americans and hold onto Beaver Dams. But Laura Secord's contribution was neither rewarded nor recognized by the Canadian government until 1885, when she received an honour from the Prince of Wales.

Each selection of chocolates was packaged in a black-and-white box decorated with a Laura Secord cameo. So it would be that O'Connor would grant Laura Secord a more lasting legacy than the Canadian government afforded such a heroine in either life or death.

Despite such refinement, O'Connor was a shameless promoter when it came to stirring up trade for his fledgling business. He is reported to have regularly walked into drug stores and loudly asked for a "pound of those lovely Laura Secord candies."

When the puzzled clerks said that they'd never heard of such chocolates, O'Connor would protest even louder that "they are the best in town. You buy them at 354 Yonge Street."

By the time the first shots of World War I were fired, Neilson's was churning out 1 million gallons of ice cream and 563,000 pounds of chocolate a year. Fruit and cough drops were also being produced. Hard candies were easier to

Berto Sobrevinas, a Phillipine-Canadian artist, holds his 23"x15" painting of the Laura Secord homestead in Queenston, from which the 8'x12' mural was electronically reproduced using a Japanese technique for the first time in Canada, 1977.

1913 hand-drawn sketch for Neilson's flavoured chocolates.

Rogers apparently planned to move into the new building in 1905 and had leased the store to a local fish and fruit merchant for the interim. But in January 1905, tragedy struck: Fredrick Morrison Rogers, Charles and Leah's only son, shot and killed himself in Victoria's New England hotel, leaving his parents a brief farewell note. The troubled boy was only fifteen.

Devastated, the couple became withdrawn almost to the point of being recluses. The move was put on hold, and the new premises were rented out to W.B. Shakespeare, a jeweller. Mr. Shakespeare's glass display cabinets, oak trim, and cupboards were ideal to display Rogers' chocolates, and remain fixtures in the Government Street location to this day.

It is said that the Rogers chocolate shop is Victoria's third largest tourist draw, after high tea at Canadian Pacific's famed Empress Hotel and a visit to the lush Butchat Gardens.

According to *Equinox*, one of the shop's most high profile visitors was an impatient Pierre Elliot Trudeau during the height of the 1980 election, when the former prime minister was fighting to get back his job. "Pierre Trudeau once stopped by while campaigning ... Just waltzed right in unannounced surrounded by all these reporters and TV cameras, and waited irritably while a panicky counter staff tried to decide what to give him."[7]

make than soft-centred chocolates and presented fewer storage problems, particularly during the hot summer months.

One day in early January 1915, William Neilson entered the factory, stumbled on a plank, and fell to the floor. Days later, on a visit to his hometown of Almonte, he suffered a paralytic stroke. On February 10, 1915, the founder of William Neilson, Limited, died at his home on Gladstone Avenue. Neilson's son Morden took over the company.

On the other side of the country, Charles and Leah Rogers' Government Street shop was no longer large enough to house the couple's growing chocolate making, retail, and mail order business. The couple had moved up the street from the original grocery in 1891. In 1917, they moved across the street to a larger brick building that Charles had built to spec in 1903.

Truth was, the shop had been too small for a long time.

The Great War was already raging across the battlefields of Europe, and Canada's confectionery industry was being propelled into a period of uncertain growth aided by advancements in automation.

World War I produced a paradox of severe shortages coupled with increased demand for chocolate. Canada has always relied on outside markets for the two primary ingredients for making chocolate: cocoa and sugar. Restrictions on imports affected the flow of these raw materials. The cost of sugar increased by two cents a pound, while cocoa doubled in price.

Many skilled and unskilled workers were sent to Europe or assigned to munitions plants and other vital wartime industries. Keeping machinery in repair and running was a constant challenge. Sharp increases in rail rates added to the confectionery industry's cost headaches. As higher commodity prices ate into profit margins, the Canadian government appealed to the industry not to cut staffing levels or wages.

But the war also created a groundswell of emotion and sentiment, with affections often being expressed through elaborately wrapped boxes of chocolates. Chocolate was also regarded as a morale booster for Canadian soldiers and was included in the care packages that families sent overseas.

Confectioners were quick to meet changes in taste with changes in production. Emphasis was shifted away from bulk chocolate and toward chocolate bars and individually wrapped chocolate products. By 1919, for example, Neilson's annual chocolate output had increased tenfold, to 5.5 million pounds.

At the heart of such unprecedented growth was the Soldier Bar. Introduced in 1914, the individually wrapped plain bar of chocolate was being produced in volume for shipment to Allied soldiers overseas.

The Soldier Bar was so popular that Neilson had to install a semi-automatic wrapping machine to bridge the gap between the company's shortage of labour and mass production of chocolate.

The war years were a crude industrial textbook in early day-to-day crisis. For Neilson, a steady stream of milk flowed from a former cheese factory in Beachville, Ontario,

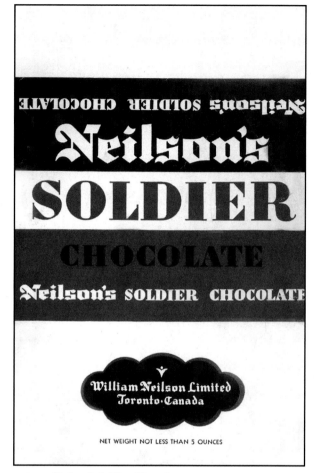

Neilson's Soldier Chocolate wrapper.

which William Neilson had bought and re-equipped in 1911. But cocoa and sugar had to be secured from a patchwork of suppliers, while a pool of less than skilled workers repaired machinery.

Morden Neilson participating in the Victory Bonds campaign.

# The Roaring Twenties

*"They're kind of an icon in Canadian retailing. There's Tim Horton, the famous Leaf hockey player and doughnut maker, and Laura Secord, cow herder and patron saint of chocolate candy in Canada."*

Retail consultant Len Kubas
talking to Canadian Press

The "roaring twenties" was a decade of expansion for the Canadian confectionery industry, although the size of the population, dispersed as it was across a huge land mass, was a problem for new entrants anxious to control costs and ship product from coast to coast.

Few confectionery companies could afford their own distribution network, and they relied for the most part on agents and wholesalers. Canada was also suffering from a post-war slump in commodity prices, resulting in over-competition, over-capacity, and a decline in consumer purchasing, which impacted on higher end candies.

These market conditions worked well for J.W. Cowan, a Toronto-based manufacturer of cheaper quality cocoa,

chocolate coatings, and bars. Cowan, founded in 1886, was Canada's largest supplier of cocoa and chocolate products. The company's Perfection brand of tinned cocoa was a particular favourite, as were their bite-sized chocolate chips known as Maple Buds. In 1920, *Western Home Monthly* declared Maple Buds Canada's favourite brand of chocolate, following a survey of readers.

Every candy bar has its own identity, created through a mix of different ingredients. Cocoa is the common denominator, followed by chewy substances such as caramel and fudge. Both have long been among the chocolatier's favourite ingredients: tasty, sticky sub-

Price lists.

stances that hold the other ingredients together before being sealed forever inside a velvety chocolate coating.

Nine years after introducing Canada's first nickel bar, Ganong wanted to put its own stamp on another distinct product — a chocolate bar that would mimic the texture of cheese: when bit into, it would be neither too firm nor too soft. It was up to candymaker Ed Bosein to create the recipe. This he did with a fudge and coconut bar surrounded by nuts and chocolate. The company was less than enthusiastic, deciding to manufacture the bar only long enough to recover its investment (if that was possible).

It was. The new bar was named Pal-O-Mine. To keep the cost of production down, Ganong decided to simply wrap the chocolate in clear cellophane recently imported from France. Even with this half-hearted attempt at promotion, Pal-O-Mine caught on, writes David Folster in his book on the Ganongs. "They loved it in Quebec, because it was so rich in sugar. They liked it a lot less in Ontario, for the same reason."

Caught by surprise, but now determined to boost sales in Ontario, Ganong began advertising Pal-O-Mine on the sides of streetcars with the slogan "Dollar Quality in 5¢ installments."

1910 advertisements for Rowntree's Elect Cocoa.

Also in 1919, J.S. Fry & Sons, which had recently merged with Cadbury in its native Great Britain, partnered with Walter Lowney of Boston in a joint venture known as the Canadian Cocoa and Chocolate Co. Ltd.

Fry had been exporting cocoa to Canada since the nineteenth century, despite high tariffs imposed on such products by the federal government in 1879. Fry was also not the only British confectioner with its eye on Canada in the 1920s.

Rowntree, a large manufacturer of cocoa, chocolate, and confectionery based in York, England, was interested in finding a Canadian partner to manufacture and distrib-

ute Chufrus, a line of fruit-flavoured gums (not to be confused with chewing gum), packaged in tubes. The company was formed when Henry Isaac Rowntree, son of a Quaker grocer, bought the cocoa, chocolate, and chicory business of his employers in 1862. Two years later, Henry purchased a local foundry and transformed it into a production facility.

The company's flagship brand was Rowntree's Prize Medal Rock Cocoa. Rock cocoa eschewed the Van Houten method of extracting cacao butter from the bean, preferring to use old technology to create a fine ground cocoa cake, mixed with sugar and more soluble when added to water.

Like J.S. Fry & Sons, Rowntree had been exporting cocoa to Canada since the late nineteenth century, and they had been represented by a sales agent in the country since the turn of the twentieth century. The company, which was also looking at partnerships in the United States, saw the Chufrus venture as the first step in market development, which, depending on sales, could lead to the local manufacture of fine ingredient chocolates.

But Canada was not a one-way street for foreign confectioners to enter. Frank O'Connor was ambitious enough to want to break into the United States. O'Connor, who was so loyal to the art of candymaking that he preferred his two manufacturing facilities in Toronto and Montreal be called

Rolling peanut brittle in the Laura Secord kitchen, 1913.

studios rather than plants, had already opened an impressive chain of Laura Secord shops in Ontario and Quebec.

In 1919, O'Connor opened his third chocolate studio in Rochester, New York. O'Connor recognized the futility of breaking into the American market using the image of an unknown Canadian heroine (who by definition would be considered an American traitor). Instead, he named the American version of his popular chocolate after Fannie Farmer, the Boston editor of a famous early American cookbook, who is reported to have revolutionized food preparation by introducing precise measurements.

Except for the name change, the American marketing approach was almost identical to the Canadian experience, selling chocolates in boxes featuring a cameo of the American culinary icon.

Hazel Kinnear, painstakingly building candy at Laura Secord.

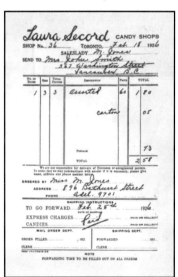

A Laura Secord order form from 1926.

By 1924, O'Connor had forty-six Laura Secord and fifty-four Fanny Farmer stores in North America, with *The Financial Post* describing him as owner of the world's largest chain of candy shops.

Amy Lustgarten, who joined Laura Secord in 1929, later told *Weekend Magazine*, "working at Laura's is a little like being brought up in a convent. The cleanliness, all the rules — but also the security and the way the executives notice if you do well."

Also in 1919, Charles Doerr signed a major contract with fellow Kitchener confectioner Hamblin Metcalf (later known as Smiles and Chuckles) to produce chocolate candies for

The Dare product range before 1916.

export to England. The deal provided Doerr with the cash he need for a massive expansion — a forty-thousand-square-foot, four-storey, steel frame addition, which doubled his floor space and left substantial room for growth.

While O'Connor and Doerr looked to export Canadian tastes to the United States, and Rowntree explored an entry into the Canadian market, William Neilson, Limited was experimenting with new products and different production methods. In 1922, the company launched North America's first dairy bar — the Eskimo Pie — by dressing up a man in a bulky Eskimo parka in mid-summer. The sweltering promoter walked up and down Yonge Street, outside of Loew's Theatre, selling Eskimo Pies to theatre patrons and passersby. The early marriage of ice cream and chocolate was formed by hand dipping bars of ice cream into vats of chocolate sauce and hanging the dripping product on wires to set.

Series of billboard ads, 1919–1923.

Hand dipping was a core business at Neilson's in the 1920s. No fewer than 120 employees were dedicated to dipping in chocolate the variety of centres that would be packaged into one of the company's popular boxed assortments. All boxes were designed and made at the plant, and they were often elaborately decorated with padded lids, ribbons, and beautiful artwork. Every year, special twelve-pound "director" boxes were sent as gifts to royalty and prime ministers.

In 1924, Morden used his flair for promotion to launch what was to become Neilson's own "flagship" chocolate bar: Jersey Milk. Stressing the "fresh milk daily" quality of the new bar, the company awarded a jersey cow to the salesman who achieved the largest num-

Displays of Neilson's Chocolate Peppermint and Caramel Rolls.

making local favourites such as Running Wild and Cherry Ripe in 1917. Seven years later, the company hit on its biggest success, a nut rolled candy bar that the company called Sweet Marie.

The bar proved to be so popular that visitors to the Willa'rds booth at the 1925 Canadian National Exhibition were fascinated to watch young women produce the caramel, fudge, peanut, and chocolate treat by hand.

Three variations of the William Neilson Peacock logo used in the 1920s.

ber of dealer sales. A photogenic cow was acquired from a farmer, presented to the winning representative, and sold back to the farm once the publicity photographs had been taken.

Neilson was not the only candymaker to introduce a new bar on the streets of Toronto in 1924. Undaunted by shortages caused by the war, Willa'rds (pronounced Will*ards*) began

Late 1920s display of Neilson products along with Canada Dry soft drinks and Kodak film.

Neilson display at the 1919 international trade show in Lyon, France.

The optimism felt by many of Canada's largest confectionery companies was not shared at J.W. Cowan. The company had invested aggressively in expansion during the economic boom that preceded World War I and was now caught in a financial squeeze. By 1924, H.N. Cowan, son of the company's founder, was looking for investment from Rowntree to launch a new line of higher quality five- and ten-cent bars to be individually wrapped and supported by national advertising.

Rowntree, which had recently renamed its Chufrus gum Chujubes in Canada and had invested over $4,000 promoting the product in Montreal, Toronto, Winnipeg, and Vancouver, was still interested in having manufacturing capacity in Canada. It is not difficult to understand why.

The Canadian subsidiary of J.S. Fry & Sons, which by this time had terminated its partnership with Lowney in the Canadian Cocoa and Chocolate Co. and was manufacturing independently in its own factory in Montreal, was dominating the cocoa market. During the 1920s, Fry would leverage its position in Canada to capture approximately 50 percent of cocoa sales.

Rowntree was interested in Cowan's factory but was reluctant to go into a partnership with a company it considered too old-fashioned and not really committed to the type of fine ingredient manufacturing that would raise the quality of its chocolate products.

The company was experiencing similar lacklustre results finding a partner in the United States. In 1925, based on an analyst's report on the American market, Rowntree began exporting Chufrus to New York, Boston, and Chicago. Sales were poor. One flaw in the marketing plan was that Americans preferred gum that they could chew for extended periods. Rowntree approached Walter Baker & Co. to enter into a joint business venture that would also distribute tubes of the eventually doomed Chufrus nationwide.

In 1924, Lowney began producing Oh Henry — a bar similar to Sweet Marie — in Canada under license from the Williamson Candy Company of Chicago. The bar was apparently named after a boy, Henry, who used to visit the Williamson factory to flirt with the young girls making the candy. The girls are said to have turned this minor distraction into an advantage by having Henry do their fetching and carrying, calling out "Oh Henry!" each time they needed something. (Interestingly, while Hershey manufactures Oh Henry in Canada, Nestlé produces the bar in the United States.)

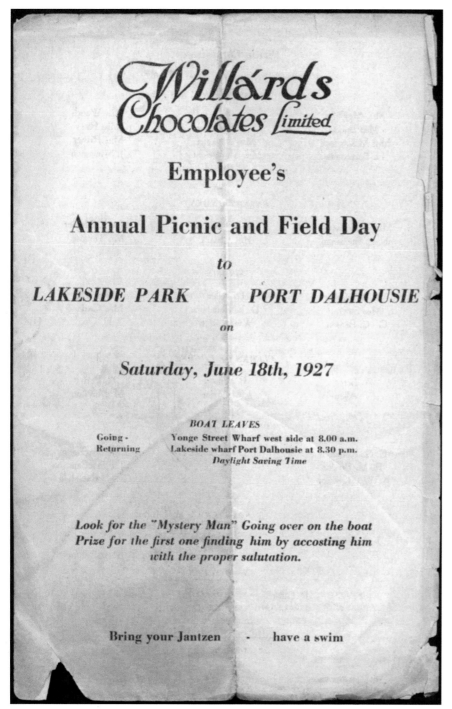

Baker's was established in 1764 in Dorchester, Massachusetts, by James Baker, a physician, and John Hannon, an Irish-American chocolate maker. The company is reported to have operated North America's first successful chocolate mill.

Negotiations between Rowntree and Baker's broke down, likely over the British company's insistence on a majority stake in any enterprise. The failure to enter into a partnership with Baker's held some significance for the Canadian confectionery industry. The American chocolatier had opened a Toronto subsidiary in the 1920s, which likely would have produced Rowntree chocolates for the Canadian market.

Instead, in October 1926, Rowntree purchased the assets of J.W. Cowan for $1 million, offering the son of the founder a small, non-voting share and a seat on the board. On January 1, 1927, Rowntree & Company was born, and the company began recasting Cowan in its own image. In retrospect, after dithering about building a physical presence in Canada since 1920, the timing could not have been worse.

Prohibition had come to Canada in 1915, with Saskatchewan becoming the first province to ban the "demon drink." On April 1, 1918, the federal government passed a law prohibiting the manufacture, importation, and transport of beverages containing more than 2.5 per-

Willa'rds Chocolates Limited's annual employee picnic flyer, 1927.

cent alcohol except in special circumstances, such as for medicinal purposes.

Unlike the United States, however, support for prohibition dissolved almost as quickly as the law was passed. In October 1920, British Columbia allowed liquor to be sold by the provincial government. The loosening of liquor consumption, however, did not prevent Hugh Forrester, owner of Purdy's, from running afoul of the law with the sale of liqueur-filled chocolates.

Purdy's was one of three Vancouver companies to brush against the Government Liquor Act by keeping "intoxicating liquor" for the purpose of sale. Forrester's contraband chocolates consisted of an outer shell in the shape of a bottle with 7.87 percent alcohol (mostly concentrated whiskey, rum, and brandy) injected into the cavity.

"During the tourist months we'd make twenty-five to thirty pounds a night and sell most of them to Americans," Forrester said after retiring in 1963.

Forrester was reportedly warned that his chocolate liqueurs might contravene government regulations, but he refused to stop, arguing that his creations were not liquor. A magistrate ruled otherwise. Purdy's was ordered to cease production and pay a $1000 fine. The decision was reversed by the British Columbia Court of Appeal in December 1926, but was upheld the following January by the Chief Justice of the Supreme Court.

Hugh Forrester's brief foray into the liquor business ended, to the disappointment of hundreds of American tourists who would have to endure the strains of prohibition for another six years, until Herbert Hoover's "noble experiment" was finally repelled.

In 1927 Moirs was booming. In an historical retrospective, *Halifax Magazine* described the mood:

> Twenty-one salesmen — decked out in felt hats and dark overcoats — got off the Ocean Limited one cold day in January for a three-day convention in Halifax. The men representing territories from Newfoundland to British Columbia were entertained at the finest hotels and restaurants, dancing to the music of the Moirs Limited orchestra, and were fired with merchandising zeal. The salesmen, many who had never before seen head office, toured the new Moirs' head office, a nine storey building boasting the most modern of confectionery manufacturing equipment.

The following year, Moirs launched its famous Pot of Gold chocolate assortment, using the XXX recipe that James Moir had developed almost half a century earlier. Each box featured a stylish young lady waiting at the end of a rainbow. It was a marketing tradition the company would update and maintain for forty-six years, with the single exception of 1962 (the year sales dropped considerably). By the time the tradition was retired for good, eighteen different young women had appeared on a Moirs Pot of Gold box.

# The Great Depression

*"We didn't make a lot of money but we had a lot of fun."*

Harold Oswin, creator of Crispy Crunch
*Toronto Star*, February 22, 1980

The stock market crash of 1929 ushered in the Great Depression and subsequent collapse of both consumer prices and demand. Canada's workforce, largely dependent on agriculture, mining and forest products, was particularly vulnerable. As the depression deepened and work camps sprung up across the country there was barely money among the general population for essentials, let alone luxury items such as chocolate and confectionery.

Interestingly, it was during the Great Depression that the seeds that would eventually lead to the globalization of much of the Canadian chocolate industry were first planted. Certainly there would be Johnny-come-latelys (Hershey in the early 1960s; Mars, first through imports from the UK and later through Effem Foods; Nestlé, already selling tins of Quick chocolate drink to Canadians, but yet to build a market in Canada for its chocolate bars similar to that which existed in the United States) but by the end of the decade, the bulk of established players in confectionery had planted their corporate colours on Canadian soil.

In the first three years of the Depression, confectionery production plunged by approximately 30 percent and the industry was drowning in a sea of red ink. Confectioners lost an estimated $1 million in 1932 alone.

Purdy's battled the Depression by staying open late each evening and offering a one-dollar special on weekends — a pound of peanut brittle and half pound of another candy.

Higher end chocolates were probably not hit as hard as they might have been because Canada was already a market that purchased gums, cocoa, and cheaper lines. Despite its reputation for quality and the aggressive promotion of an extensive line of higher quality products, Cowan's cheaper lines accounted for approximately 95 percent of Rowntree sales in 1927, and more than 98 percent of sales one year later.

Cocoa product display from the 1930s and 1940s.

Rowntree had also miscalculated by taking Cowan's Perfection cocoa off the market to build market share for its higher end brands. Rowntree ended up losing more of the market to Fry's and was forced to retreat and return Perfection to store shelves.

It appeared that nobody would be spared. Overnight, the Depression altered the fortunes of candymakers like Doerr, who shifted from a quarter of a century of rapid growth into a decade-long period of stagnation. Annual sales dropped from $300,000 to $120,000 and held at that level through the 1930s. There was no money for reinvestment, and the entire fourth floor of the plant remained empty. The company was barely getting by.

At Ganong, sales also plummeted. Prior to the Depression, Ganong routinely crammed four railway boxcars full of candy every autumn just to keep up with the T.

The morning after the Great Fire at Dare, February 1943.

Eaton's Company mail order business. By 1932, the candymaker had lost more than 50 percent of its pre-Depression sales. The sales branch in crowded Toronto was closed. Wages were slashed, the workforce was cut, and Christmas bonuses were cancelled for the first time in thirty years. Arthur Ganong reduced his own salary by 15 percent before taking a second cut of 18 percent.

At least two major companies introduced new products on the eve of the Depression and during its first months.

The *Mail and Empire*, October 2, 1930. Promoting a Neilson's concert series on CKNC and CFRB featuring the Jersey Milk Chocolate Orchestra.

Since 1923, William Neilson, Limited had been selling bite-sized pieces of a chocolate-covered peanut butter bar. Harold Oswin, a candy roller in Neilson's Hard Candy Room who had joined the company when he was fourteen years old, had developed the candy.

The candy consisted of peanut butter tucked inside a bright yellow jacket of blended sugar, molasses, and vanilla, then dunked in chocolate. The final product provided a unique taste that was both moist and crisp.

Oswin, who was promoted to candymaker in the late 1920s, had wanted to produce his creation in a round format similar to Neilson's chocolate-covered peppermint and

1935 advertisement from *The Voyageur* promoting Burnt Almond French Style Chocolate.

cherry bars. Neilson's management opted for a flat bar, and the reformatted chocolate bar was marketed as Crispy Crunch in 1930.

The Curtiss Candy Company had introduced a similar product in the United States in 1926. Curtiss had introduced the Baby Ruth bar (named after President Grover Cleveland's daughter and not the famous New York Yankee baseball player) six years earlier.[8] The company sold its peanut butter candy in bar form, naming it Butterfinger.

Rowntree launched fruit pastilles to the North American market in 1929. Sales for pastilles were slightly better than Chufrus/Chujubes, but remained far below expectation. Meanwhile, across the Atlantic, another chocolate giant was beginning to stir.

In 1824, John Cadbury, another British Quaker, had opened a small grocery in the heart of Birmingham, England's most prestigious shopping district. The grocery sold both coffee and tea (Cadbury hired a gentleman of Chinese descent to work behind the counter in authentic costume), but the young merchant was anxious to promote his line of cocoa and chocolate drinks.

In the March 1, 1824 edition of the *Birmingham Gazette*, he advertised that "John Cadbury is desirous of introducing to particular notice 'Cocoa Nibs', prepared by himself, an article affording a most nutritious beverage for breakfast."

In 1831, a small factory was rented to produce cocoa and chocolate beverages, and within ten years, chocolate was Cadbury's business; he sold sixteen types of drinking chocolate and eleven cocoas.

The British market, which has traditionally influenced Canadian tastes, was very competitive in the latter half of the nineteenth century. J.S. Fry & Sons was the sole supplier of chocolate and cocoa to the Royal Navy. The navy contract propelled the confectioner into the desirable position as the largest chocolate manufacturer in the world.

Cadbury scored its own marketing coup in 1853, as purveyors of chocolate to Queen Victoria. In 1866 the company purchased a van Houten cocoa press and began selling its own Cadbury's Cocoa Essence. Even with the popularity of its cocoa in its home market, Cadbury, unlike Fry and Rowntree, choose not to export the product to Canada.

Cadbury's early interest in North America was confined to the United States. But the company concluded that twentieth-century America was already well served by domestic producers such as Hershey and Mars. The required investment for Britain's largest chocolate maker to penetrate this market was considered too great. But the company viewed Canada differently.

The J.S. Fry Canada subsidiary in Montreal was profitable but underdeveloped. Fry's cocoa was already the country's best-selling brand. Ironically, the company credited with having produced the world's first eating chocolate remained under-represented in the manufacture and sale of chocolate bars.

In 1930, Cadbury assumed control of the Montreal plant. The company decided to arrive in Canada with a splash by investing £80,000 to expand the facility and launch its Dairy Milk bar. Dairy Milk had been introduced in England in 1905 to counter demand for the milk chocolate bars that were coming across the Channel from Switzerland. Three names, including Dairy Maid and Highland Milk, were considered before Cadbury settled on the hybrid Dairy Milk.

Dairy Milk quickly overtook Neilson's Jersey Milk as Canada's best-selling milk chocolate bar. Both products eclipsed Rowntree's York Milk, which, along with Chufrus and pastilles, struggled to gain a toehold in the Canadian market.

Rowntree experienced greater success with toffees. In 1931, the company entered into a licensing agreement with Halifax, England-based John Mackintosh & Sons, Limited to manufacture and distribute its product line in Toronto. Unknown to the company at the time, it was also on the brink of bringing to Canada what would turn out to be some of this country's best-selling chocolate bars.

Desperate to gain ground lost in its home market to Cadbury's Dairy Milk, Rowntree began test-marketing a new aerated, bubbly milk chocolate bar in Northern England in 1935. The new bar was called Aero, and within one month of its release it appeared to beat out Dairy Milk two to one in terms of consumer preference.

Alongside Aero, Rowntree also launched a chocolate-covered wafer bar called Chocolate Crisp (after a brief experiment with the equally uninspiring brand name Wafer Crisp).

Rowntree was buoyed by the overnight success of both Aero and Chocolate Crisp at home, but remained hesitant over how the two bars would be received in the Canadian market, now steadily recovering from the Depression. There was also some consideration given to marketing both lines in the United States, where American giant Hershey controlled approximately two-thirds of the chocolate bar market.

Whether this renewed interest in the United States would have been accomplished by exporting Canadian-made products was not clear. Rowntree sold the patent to manufacture Aero in the U.S. to Hershey in May 1937, three months before deciding go ahead with the manufacture of the aerated bar and Chocolate Crisp at the company's plant in Toronto.

Canadians got their first bite of Aero and Biscrisp (the name given to the Canadian version of Chocolate Crisp) in

Advertising Coffee Crisp.

the autumn of 1937. Early reaction was favourable. Twenty years later, Rowntree would broaden the appeal of Aero in England by introducing peppermint, orange, and coffee versions of the same bar — but not before the Canadian operation had added coffee to a hybrid version of Aero and Biscrisp to produce Coffee Crisp, which the company launched in 1938.

The Scottish Highlands of 1938 became the testing ground for a new panned chocolate "bean" aimed at children. The beans, first sold loose and later marketed in tubes, contained a soft chocolate centre encased in a crispier chocolate shell and covered in a multicoloured sugar coating.

Scottish consumers reacted favourably to the candy, which the manufacturer, Rowntree, was selling as Smarties Chocolate Beans.

# World War II

World War II was a period of great shortages, but with even greater marketing opportunities once hostilities ceased. During the seven-year conflict, the chocolate bar and, to a lesser extent, sugar-based candy had grown up. The advertising industry promoted the image of chocolate as the food that provided energy to Canadian soldiers.

In retrospect it was a renewed emphasis on a fairly ancient theme. The Aztecs were also familiar with the energy-boosting properties of chocolatl and permitted their warriors to partake of the drink otherwise reserved for the ruling elite and those they favoured. In 1528, Hernán Cortés calculated that a warrior could go an entire day without food after drinking a single cup of chocolate.

Chocolate, like Neilson's Soldier bar, was also a mainstay of army ration packs during the Great War. On this occasion, candy producers appeared more willing to promote the food that had fuelled the appetites of the military.

In the United States, for example, the National Confectioners Association of America poured $1 million into a 1944 campaign to promote the link between candy and those brave American GIs.

Typically, Canadian efforts were more subdued. But the underlying message appeared to resonate: candy was no longer for children. Indeed, a spin-off effect was to occur as soldiers returned home with an appreciation for chocolate and a hunger for more (there were stories of servicemen gobbling up the bars of chocolate once they were handed their ration pack).

But before Canada's confectionery industry could cash in on the spoils of war, it had to struggle through the severe shortages caused by the conflict — most notably in commodities, such as sugar and cocoa, and in skilled labour.

Parliament approved going to war against Germany on September 9, 1939, (King George VI formally declaring war on Canada's behalf in London the very next day). During the early months of war, Canada would escape the shortages that plagued manufacturers and consumers across the Atlantic.

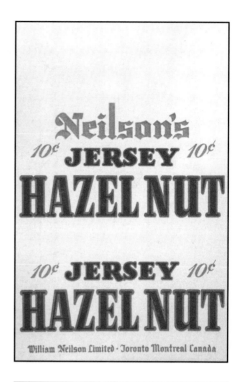

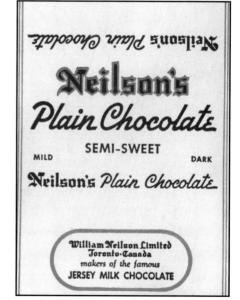

Neilson's wrappers continued to develop in the 1940s.

But the economic stimulation of war — spurred by massive government spending and extensive wartime manufacturing — created an artificial economy for a country that had not fully recovered from the Depression. Unemployment fell rapidly as Canadian men shipped out to Europe and those left behind began to build airplanes, tanks, and munitions to support the war effort.

Canadians once again had money to spend, but fewer and fewer items to spend it on. Suppliers, merchants, and farmers were taking advantage of supply and demand. By 1941, inflation was running at 6 percent.

A young boy in Athens selling a Neilson's chocolate bar previously distributed free in Canadian Red Cross parcels, 1945.

Worried over the potential for runaway inflation, William Lyon Mackenzie King's Liberal government created the Wartime Prices and Trade Board in February 1941. Central control over the Canadian economy had begun in earnest.

The Board immediately imposed a general ceiling on prices, wages, and rents. Goods such as gasoline and sugar were rationed. And the government banned the import of commodities such as cocoa powder in an effort to preserve precious shipping space for essentials that could not be readily produced here.

However, this imposition proved to be something of a boon for indigenous manufacturers of cocoa. Rowntree, for one, opted to expand its Toronto operation.

Still, controls on essential ingredients conflicted with the surge in demand for chocolate to be exported to Western Europe and Asia. Initiatives such as the 1942 subsidy on cocoa softened some of the challenges faced by confectioners, but other problems, such as sugar rationing and human resources, remained.

The uninterrupted flow of sugar was one of the industry's biggest headaches. "In the war years when sugar was rationed, [Purdy's would] open at noon and there'd be line-ups down the block. We'd be sold out in half an hour, even limiting customers to a pound each," said Hugh Forrester.

Quotas were based on the previous year's usage. In a letter to his son Graham, Morden Neilson described the difficulty that the company was experiencing securing supplies as late as 1945:

The effects of the war are not yet over. Europe has to be fed and one result is

1940s advertisement for Neilson's Jersey Brand Cocoa.

Above all, confectionery was business, and business has an inherent ability to try to manipulate events to secure market advantage. War, and the groundswell of Canadian patriotism, proved to be no exception. In the rawest form, entrepreneurs profited from the black market by selling unused ration coupons.

Other attempts to take advantage of market conditions were less blunt. Rationing was taking a toll. By 1942, manufacturers were culling their lines. Ganong reduced production to four bars, including the surprisingly popular Pal-O-Mine. Rowntree temporarily suspended manufacture of Aero, Chocolate Crisp, and its homegrown favourite, Coffee Crisp. The company also abandoned plans to produce Licorice All-Sort in Canada under license from Bassett's in the UK.

Multinationals fared worse than Canadian producers; the ban on confectionery imports meant that neither Rowntree nor Cadbury could compensate reductions in Canadian manufacturing by stocking store shelves with bars imported from Great Britain.

Fewer chocolate bars did not dampen Canadians' appetite for chocolate. The friendly corner store operator was helpless: unable to satisfy consumer demand, but prevented from controlling consumption (and improving margins) by raising prices. Many retailers resorted to hiding chocolate bars under the counter, the same way they would conceal contraband cigarettes and pornography.

Demand for chocolate bars was outstripping all other types of confectionery, including boxed chocolate selections, and Canada's largest manufacturers of bars were quick to seize upon this.

Not too long after it had been created, several of Canada's largest chocolate companies approached the Wartime Prices and Trade Board with a plan in which the industry would pump all its rationed sugar and cocoa into producing chocolate bars. This threatened the existence of competitors such as Ganong and Moirs, whose product

a further cut in the use of sugar. For the most part we have been allowed 70 percent of 1941 use. At the moment it is 65 percent and we are told it will be 50 percent.

You can easily imagine what that may mean to our business. On the other hand we are likely to receive large orders for chocolate bars and cocoa for overseas shipment to Europe and free sugar will be allowed for that so you see there usually is a silver lining to clouds.

lines were dominated by confections other than chocolate bars. Nevertheless, the Board agreed.

This remained unacceptable to Whidden Ganong, who sat on the Board as the Maritime confectionery representative. Perhaps thinking back to when his grandfather and great-uncle entered into a price war with Charles Holt in the nineteenth century, Ganong threatened to destabilize prices by selling his chocolate bars at one cent lower than the rest of the industry.

Only one-third of Ganong's production was in chocolate bars. Even if the company poured its entire cocoa and sugar ration into bars, it was unlikely that Ganong could gain a worthwhile share of a market already dominated by the big three. Still, the industry could not ignore the impact such a cut would have on revenues. The Board relented.

The situation contrasted sharply with the fortunes of William Neilson Limited, which was the only Canadian candy manufacturer to process cocoa beans to make the chocolate liquor that formed the base of chocolate production.

The cocoa roasting facility was, at one point, on the fourth floor of the Gladstone plant, where Amos Steele, a supervisor and notorious cigar smoker, would subject random bins of beans to the aroma test. Amos would roll his trademark stogy to the side of his mouth while inhaling a handful of cocoa beans. The aroma of the bean would tell him whether or not they were ready. The cigar, Amos convinced management, helped to keep his nose keen.

By the end of the war, Neilson had gained ground in the domestic market as Canada's largest manufacturer of confectionery.

Displaying the variety of Neilson's candies.

Neilson's delivery trucks, circa 1940s.

# Post-war Expansion 10

*"St. Stephen's foremost subject of speculation is how to get every Canadian to eat one more piece of candy. So far, nobody has come up with the answer, but if anybody ever does the town that lives on candy will be a bigger and busier place."*

Ian Sclanders
*Maclean's*, December 24, 1955

The war ended in 1945. But the government did not dissolve the Wartime Prices and Trade Board right away. The Board had succeeded in keeping inflation in check. Between October 1941 and April 1945, prices rose in Canada by 3.8 percent — the pace of such increases was approximately 33 percent lower than the year-to-year rate of inflation the government faced in 1941 when it first created the Board.

The government believed that the economy still needed to be managed to prevent wild wage and price increases after four years of tight controls. For the next six years, ceilings on prices and salaries were gradually eliminated.

In early 1947, it was the confectionery industry's turn. Manufacturers responded by boosting the price of a five-cent chocolate bar 60 percent to eight cents. Manufacturers justified the increase by pointing to the loss of lucrative wartime contracts, an end to the cocoa subsidy, and the rise in costs of everything from packaging to labour.

As the once empty candy counters of war-depressed merchants were re-stocked with eight-cent chocolate bars, Canada's youngest consumers made a call to arms in what Calgary writer Yanick LeClerc describes as the war of the nickel bar.[9]

The war began innocently enough. On April 25, 1947, a small band of outraged adolescent activists on Vancouver Island staged protests in front of local candy stores with signs urging the boycott of the eight-cent bar.

By the time the revolt ended less than two weeks later, the battle had spread like brush fire across the country. Beleagured candymakers were on the defensive, one legislature was ground to a halt, and a labour movement was discredited. Meanwhile, the *Toronto Telegram*, one of Canada's

Protesting the rise in chocolate prices.

largest and most conservative newspapers, was shamelessly engaged in Cold War rhetoric.

In the mid-1950s, consumption in Canada appeared to be on the verge of a breakthrough. It was a welcome change for confectioners, who continued to watch candy sales stagnate while other food industries were chalking up impressive gains.

Canadian consumption lagged behind both the United States and Great Britain — two markets that were considered a natural measure of industry performance, given the similarities of the population and the influence each country had on the Canadian industry. Canadians were eating fourteen pounds of candy per year, overshadowed by the seventeen pounds in the United States, and absolutely dwarfed by the twenty-eight pounds of sweets per person being "scarfed down" in the U.K.

There were concerns that a disproportionate bite of that fourteen pounds was being supplied by British and European importers, taking advantage of favourable exchange rates. The biggest problem, however, was more domestic than international. Governments continued to tax confectionery as a luxury item. This conflicted with the practices of other countries that considered confectionery a food, exempt from taxes.

In the 1930s, Arthur Ganong, also a Conservative member of parliament in the early depression government of R.B. Bennett, refused to return to his seat until the prime minister agreed to cut in half a 2 percent tax added to the price of sugar.

courtesy of Ganong Bros., Ltd.

Arthur Ganong.

courtesy of Ganong Bros., Ltd.

Wrapping Pepts in the bar wrapping department, 1940.

But while the industry may have been the victor in small skirmishes, the government continued to roll over the market with excessive levels of taxation that often turned regional favourites into casualties of war.

Ganong's popular roll of chocolate-covered soft mint centres was one such casualty. Pepts were introduced by Ganong in 1925, and closely resembled today's Rolo. In fact, Ganong would later expand the line to include Car-mels, with a soft caramel centre.

Pepts also gave the Ganong family the flexibility to adapt the size of the roll to commodity prices and other economic influences. So much so that David Folster described Pepts as a "kind of yardstick on the state of the Canadian economy." During the Depression, when cocoa beans sold for four and a half cents a pound, Ganong's was able to pack twelve pieces into the five-cent Pepts roll and still make money. On other occasions, consumers would open the Pepts foil wrapper to find only ten pieces.

Ganong temporarily suspended Pepts during World War II, returning the candy to production in 1948 when rations of sugar and cocoa were lifted. In 1950, the federal government imposed a 30 percent excise tax on confectionery.

Overnight, the Liberal government of Louis St. Laurent had accomplished what years of wartime shortages and rationing had failed to do. Ganong would have to reduce a roll of Pepts to seven pieces in order to keep the price of the candy under a nickel. Pepts was experiencing a 17 percent surge in sales on the eve of the latest tax increase. After the tax was imposed, candy sales declined, and the Pepts line was silenced.

"It was one of the greatest pieces of bad luck that we ever suffered," Whidden Ganong would say later.

In 1956, on the verge of a significant market rise fuelled by lower commodity prices, the message from Canada's confectionery industry was clear. Lift taxes or watch the industry stagnate.

The government had already reduced the excise tax to 10 percent, but when added to a 10 percent sales tax, it still forced manufacturers to increase the price of a box of chocolates while reducing the size of nickel and dime bars. It was estimated that each ten-cent bar was only delivering eight cents of candy.

"Manufacturers cut their profit on the five cent bars and have done so to help keep the nickel alive, as it is a valuable coin in Canada," Sydney J. Smith, president of Neilson's told the Financial Post. "Abolition of the two taxes would put the confectionery industry on an equal footing with other Canadian food manufacturers as well as its foreign competition."[10]

By 1972, the tax issue appeared ready to boil over. Taxation plus rising commodity prices had already killed off the nickel bar and had sent the ten-cent bar toward the fifteen-cent mark. It may seem laughable today, as PST and GST have pushed the chocolate bar across the one dollar threshold at many retailers, but it was a serious problem for chocolate makers, especially given the uneven application of the tax.

Chocolate and soft drink manufacturers were hit. Cookies, potato chips, and other snack items that used similar ingredients were not. "People now feel they get more value from a large tin of cookies, which costs less than a pound box of chocolates, or from a bag of potato chips, which is bigger than a chocolate bar," said Cyril Balman, general manager of the Confectionery Association of Canada.

Peter Rogers, vice-president of production for Laura Secord explained the problem. "Other products, such as cereal or detergents, can shift slightly in price and it won't be noticed. But the ten-cent bar is a fixed entity in people's minds, and they don't want to pay more."

Laura Secord would later retail boxes of chocolate in drugstores across Canada.

Hershey was a latecomer to Canada, arriving in the railway junction of Smith Falls, Ontario, in 1963. Hershey told the *Financial Post* that it had waited twenty-five years for a real crack at the $100 million-a-year Canadian-manufactured-confection business.

While many were concerned over Hershey's size and marketing muscle, some manufacturers considered the American company a powerful ally in the double-edged challenge of increasing Canada's per capita consumption of chocolate and pressuring the federal government to ease or remove the tax burden.

The company's early experience north of the border would turn out to be as bitter as the famous nickel bar first introduced to Americans by the company's beloved founder, Milton Hershey. Hershey had completed a market analysis and was motivated by the pockets of acceptance some Canadians had for the unique taste of Hershey chocolate even without a national sales force or distribution network. They would soon learn that there is a world of difference between selling a trailer of chocolate in a year and running a complete production line. Hershey executives thought otherwise, believing that the only thing holding Hershey back in Canada was the bar's lack of availability.

According to local historians in the town of Smith Falls, two Hershey Food representatives were driving down Main Street in the early 1960s, scouting locations for the company's first manufacturing plant outside the United States. Spotting the Pennsylvania license plate, Smith Falls' chief of police is said to have flagged down the vehicle and begun promoting the merits of the town. Even if true, it is likely that access to fresh milk and water, excellent transport links, and close proximity to Canada's two largest markets likely influenced Hershey's decision more than an enthusiastic police chief.

The move to Canada was aggressive. A 200,000-square-foot plant capable of producing an equivalent number of five-cent and ten-cent chocolate bars a day opened in 1963. Hershey Pennsylvania had researched how the two major British players, Cadbury and Rowntree, had built up distribution in Canada and so they hired a sales force of 114 people. Cases of Hershey bars, instant chocolate, cocoa, chocolate chips, and chocolate syrup were sent to grocery, candy, and drug stores across the country.

Hershey executives went on record to say that differences in the Canadian market would guide the company's marketing approach. Unfortunately, the company refused to take the same approach when it came to their recipes.

The problem was, Canadians already accustomed to British-style sweet chocolate (especially in Quebec, where the sweeter the better) did not like the bitter taste of the Hershey bar. They were not alone. Hans Scheu, a Swiss national and former president of the Cocoa Merchants Associations, has accused Milton Hershey of "completely [ruining] the American palate with his sour gritty chocolate."

Hershey had been warned. But management could not be convinced that even with a sophisticated distribution network, Hershey chocolate would not receive the same level of consumer acceptance in Canada that it enjoyed in the United States.

"They were trying to push a piece of string for quite a while," said one retired Canadian candy executive who admits to enjoying the original Hershey chocolate recipe. By accident, Hershey Canada began pulling a new product along at approximately the same time.

In 1926, Harry Burnett Reese, a former dairyman for the Hershey Farms, opened his own chocolate plant down the road from the Hershey operation. In 1941, Reese introduced a milk-chocolate-covered peanut butter cup, which he sold for a penny. The Reese's Peanut Butter Cup was first intended to reduce the company's exposure to shortages in sugar. The candy proved to be such a hit, however, that Reese discontinued all other lines.

Still, peanut butter cups were not enough to keep the plant going. In June 1963, Hershey bought Reese, and they began manufacturing Peanut Butter Cups for the Canadian market in the Smith Falls plant two years later.

For Canadians, the Reese's Peanut Butter Cup was a welcome break from the strict adherence to Milton Hershey's original chocolate recipe, and the candy sold quite well. Curiously, another eighteen years would pass before Hershey Canada reworked its formula to manufacture the smoother, sweeter chocolate more suitable to Canadian tastes.

It should be noted that after World War I there were forty thousand different candy bars manufactured in the United States to feed soldiers who had enjoyed their first bite of chocolate in ration packs.

Post-World War II prosperity and the arrival of the first wave of baby boomers had a strong impact on growth in the candy industry, particularly with American sugar imports such as Pez and Tootsie Rolls.

What are Smarties? Ask most Canadians and we would describe Smarties as rounded pieces of chocolate coated in a thin, coloured candy shell. But ask Americans the same question and you will get a completely different answer.

Conversely, ask most Canadians to describe the candy Rockets and you are just as likely to draw a blank as an answer, even though the pastel-coloured compressed sugar tablets remain one of Canada's most popular candies (especially at Halloween, when a trick or treat bag is typically loaded with large and small rolls of cellophane-wrapped Rockets).

Indeed, the candy has been a Canadian tradition since 1964. Like so many of Canada's favourites, the launch of Rockets can be traced to England, to Swizzels Limited, a manufacturer of fizzy compressed candy tablets.

Swizzels was founded in 1933 by David Dee and Alfred and Maurice Matlow. The Matlow brothers had been manufacturing jelly confections in a small factory in London since 1928. Canadians will be most familiar with Swizzels' Love Hearts: rolls of multicoloured compressed candy tablets, each containing a raised slogan framed inside an outlined heart. According to Swizzels, today's Love Hearts contain more than two hundred phrases such as "I Love You" and "Be Mine."

Following the Second World War, Swizzels' two founding families decided to expand the business by setting up a manufacturing plant in the United States. Dee was one of two sets of brothers dispatched to New Jersey in the late 1940s to organize and run the American operation. The relationship between the Dee and Matlow brothers was strained from the beginning.

Acrimony forced Dee out of the company in the 1950s. Rather than return to England, Dee founded Ce De Candy Inc., a direct competitor that began producing rolls of compressed candy tablets that he named Smarties, the name that Rowntree had given its tubes of candy-coated chocolate beans.

"We've always been puzzled why Rowntree would copyright the Smarties name in every country around the world, except in the States," Dee said during a visit to his Canadian plant.

In 1964, Dee opened his Canadian plant inside an old factory on Toronto's Queen Street. Unable to import the Smarties name into Canada, Dee decided to let his customers name the candy rolls.

"That's why the Rockets name is not as familiar in Canada as Smarties is in the United States," explained Cyril Wolfe, President of Ce De Candy in Canada. "For the first twenty years we would print whatever the customer wanted on the wrapper."

There are conflicting stories that Smarties were the inspiration for M&Ms, which Mars first introduced in the United States in 1940. The claim is aggressively denied by Mars, although there is evidence that Forrest Mars, the frugal, driven owner (and patriarch) of family-owned Mars, and George Harris, head of Rowntree, did know each other and were even considered by some to be friends. So much so, in fact, that according to British lecturer and author Robert Fitzgerald, Forrest Mars had already travelled north to Toronto during the war to consult with and provide advice to Rowntree management, who were preparing their plant to manufacture Smarties in Canada.[11]

Mars was willing to enter into a production agreement with the British confectioner: Rowntree would join Mars in a joint venture in the United States in exchange for manufacturing Maltesers for the Canadian market. Mars had previously introduced the chocolate-covered malted balls, which were an imitation of American Whoppers, to the British market with considerable success.

Neither arrangement came to pass, the joint venture being blocked by the British government's embargo on the transfer of capital, although Rowntree would later produce under license a version of Mars's self-named Mars Bar, with the name Milky Way.

**Everyone's buying our 15¢ bars. So as an introduction to our great new 15¢ rolls, we think you deserve a special deal.**

The special deal is simply this: from April 7 to May 19, we'll be packaging 27-roll boxes of Peppermint and Caramel Rolls, but only charging you for 24.

That means you get three free rolls. (If you add it up you'll find there's an extra 45¢ profit on each box.)

Remember, stock up on our new 15¢ Peppermint and Caramel Rolls. And get in on our 27-for-the-price-of-24-roll offer.

It's a little special deal we think you deserve.

This is just one way Neilson's is going to help you Put on a Happy in 1969.

VB-1045

Trade advertisement from *Drug Merchandising* of April 1969, offering 27-roll boxes of Peppermint and Caramel Rolls for the price of 24.

# Special Occasions 11

Candy canes and foil-wrapped chocolate saints. Department stores converting their candy departments into chocolate villages elaborately decorated with stacks of gold boxes accented by bright red ribbon, coloured balls, and sprigs of holiday foliage. Heart-shaped boxes of candy. Costumed kids stuffing bags to overflowing every thirty-first of October, and baskets full of chocolate eggs and a centrepiece bunny at Easter.

Confectionery has gently worked its way into the heart of most celebrations. Giving chocolate as a gift dates back to the Aztecs. Queen Victoria

Christmas postcard for specially wrapped Neilson's boxed chocolates.

sent over two thousand kilograms of chocolate to British troops at Christmas.

Canadians do not have any truly indigenous candy customs for holidays. All ours have been imported from other countries and cultures, although a Christmas stocking filled with Ganong Chicken Bones, or a Laura Secord butter-cream egg at Easter have coloured some of our most cherished holiday memories and traditions with a distinct Canadian flavour.

Nevertheless, it is interesting to trace the origins of our holiday candy traditions. Traditional Canadian holidays such as Easter and Christmas are a mix of Christianity and pagan ritual. Not surprisingly, many stories, such as the evolution of the candy cane, are a blend of legend and more recent history.

According to the American-based National Confectioners Association, the candy cane can be traced back to Germany in 1670. The choirmaster at the Cologne Cathedral handed out sugar sticks to his young singers to keep them quite during the long Living Creche ceremony.

1940 Easter display.

In the 1920s, Bob McCormick, a candymaker in Albany, Georgia, began making candy canes as special Christmas treats for his children, friends, and local shopkeepers. It was a laborious process — pulling, twisting, cutting, and bending each stick of candy by hand. Transporting the delicate candy also posed a problem.

In the 1950s, Bob's brother-in-law, a Catholic priest, invented a machine to automate candy cane production. Packaging innovations by the younger McCormicks made it possible to transport candy canes on a larger scale.

The Cadbury Trebor Allan plant in Hamilton, Ontario produces approximately 150 million candy canes a year of various thickness, sizes, colours, and flavours. The company's British parent, Cadbury Schweppes, owns Orange Crush, Crush cream soda, and Hires root beer. The Canadian subsidiary has been engaged in a bit of cross branding by incorporating those flavours into candy canes.

Home to what was once the largest candy cane in the world (the current record holder is thirty-six feet high), the Hamilton plant produces approximately 90 percent of the candy canes licked in Canada, with the remainder going to export.

The choirmaster is said to have insisted that the candy sticks be bent to represent the shepherds' crook, an ancient symbol representing the humble shepherds who were the first to worship the newborn Christ.

Another story suggests that early German candy canes were actually glass canes filled with coloured candy, and were used to defend against witches. A person threatened by a witch would crack the cane and escape while the witch collected the candies spilling from the broken glass.

But it wasn't until the turn of the century that the red and white stripes and peppermint flavouring were added to the candy cane. The body of the cane is white, representing the life that is pure. The broad red stripe is supposed to symbolize the Lord's sacrifice for mankind.

A second Christmas tradition, far more popular in Canada than in the United States, is the Christmas cracker, invented in England in 1847 for the purpose of selling more candy.

Tom Smith, a London confectioner specializing in ornamental confections and cake decorations, began selling

Celebrating spring at Laura Secord.

Celebrating the holiday season with chocolate.

bon bons — French sugared almonds individually wrapped in coloured tissue paper — following a trip to Paris in 1840. Sales were brisk at Christmas and soft (to non-existent) the remainder of the year. Smith had already improved on the original idea by tucking a love motto into the tissue. What he wanted was another gimmick to increase sales during the busy Christmas period.

Smith decided to insert bon bons and a motto inside a small cardboard tube covered by a brightly coloured twist of paper. Inspired the crackle of the fire, he went on to develop a cracking mechanism that would "pop" when the

wrapping was broken.

So popular were Smith's crackers that special versions were created to celebrate everything from war heroes to the Coronation. Love verses were gradually replaced with bad jokes and cheap tissue paper hats, and the bon bon eventually gave way to small toys and such.

Crackers were not the only holiday treat to contain trinkets. In 1931, J.S. Fry & Sons (a division of Cadbury since 1919) launched an unusual Easter line that consisted of a chocolate egg attached to every conceivable gift item including watches, jewelry, penknives, and kitchen utensils. It was a new twist on an old custom that dated back to Victorian times where satin-covered cardboard eggs were filled with Easter gifts and chocolates. Of course, the egg as a symbol of Easter dates much further back.

Easter, like Christmas, has become a colourful blend of Christian beliefs and pagan rituals. The Easter egg, for example, owes its existence more to the pagan rites of spring than to the death and resurrection of Jesus.

Northern Europeans have held festivals to celebrate the arrival of spring for centuries. The term Easter originates from *Ostara*, the ancient Anglo Saxon goddess of dawn or rebirth.

Ancient cultures used the purity of the egg to symbolize the rebirth of nature. Bird's eggs were often given as gifts — a tradition that was enhanced during the Middle Ages by painting eggs in bright colours to represent the upcoming spring. As Christianity spread across Europe, the church exploited many of these customs for its own purpose. The egg came to symbolize the rebirth of man.

In the seventeenth and eighteenth centuries, egg-shaped toys were given to children along with other Easter gifts. A German book dating back to 1682 told the story of a rabbit (an ancient symbol of fertility) laying the eggs and hiding them in the garden. Hence the birth of the *Oschter Haws*, or Easter Bunny.

Creating Easter magic at the Laura Secord factory.

It was inevitable that somebody would consider making an egg from chocolate. The Germans and French are reported to be the first manufacturers of chocolate Easter eggs in the nineteenth century. These eggs were solid and difficult to manufacture because chocolate did not flow easily into a mould.

As the process of chocolate egg making improved and the manufacture of hollow eggs (originally produced one at a time using a chocolate paste) became less labourious, confectioners went about adding value to their Easter creations. The smooth surface of the egg was enhanced with piping chocolate and marzipan flowers.

Wrapping brightly coloured pieces of tinfoil around the chocolate continued the ancient tradition of colouring eggs. The Laura Secord Buttercream Egg was first introduced in the 1920's, and has since become a Canadian tradition for families. Indeed, some families are beginning to introduce their fourth generation to the dark chocolate egg with the buttercream centre.

Several years after Laura Secord's original buttercream egg became a fixture in Easter baskets across Canada, the company introduced the Superior Cream Egg with a chocolate cream and chopped cashew centre. Except for sizes, Laura Secord would not extend the cream egg line for approximately 50 years, when it launched the Crunchy Peanut Butter Egg with chopped peanuts and crisps.

In the 1920s and 1930s, Laura Secord timed the release of its eggs to coincide with the Easter season. As with the Cadbury Creme Egg, Laura Secord now meets demand by getting a jump on the Easter bunny. Production of buttercream eggs begins in early January, using the same recipe first developed in the 1920s. The company estimates that it now produces over $5 million worth of buttercream eggs, along with over four million foil-wrapped eggs.

Perhaps one of the most significant events in the Easter egg market occurred in the early 1950s when a carton designer, William T. Horry, revolutionized the business. Prior to this time, chocolate eggs were fragile and expensive to make and pack. While working on a carton design for a light bulb, William T. Horry realized the potential of a similar carton to hold fragile chocolate Easter eggs, and this changed the whole face of the market. The carton provided space for new bright designs and significant Easter egg branding.

Also in the 1950s, fully automatic chocolate egg machines meant that for the first time, mould heating, depositing the liquid chocolate, rotating the moulds to achieve uniform thickness, cooling, and demoulding the two halves of the egg took place in a series of mechanical operations.

While very much a product for adults in the 1920s and 1930s, mass-produced Easter eggs have paved the way for the commercialization of Easter, with an emphasis on children. Chocolate eggs are bigger and more elaborately decorated. Shell eggs containing bite-sized pieces of contemporary chocolate bars have become a major Easter favourite.

In 1971, Cadbury launched the popular Easter Creme Egg, an updated version of a cream-filled egg that the company introduced in 1923. Today Cadbury manufactures over 300 million Easter Creme Eggs, of which one-third are for export.

For centuries chocolate has been considered an aphrodisiac capable of unlocking the most deeply felt passions. Casanova is said to have considered hot chocolate the "elixer of love," preferring that beverage to champagne. Given such sensual pleasure, it is only natural that chocolate should be at the heart of Valentine's Day.

Purdy's estimates that worldwide, 10 billion conversation hearts are made on Valentine's Day, with such long-standing sayings printed on them as "Be Mine," "Be Good," and "Be True."

In Canada, the February fourteenth celebration of love accounts for approximately 10 percent of the $1.8 billion Canadians spend on confectionery each year. Approximately $12 million is spent on boxes of chocolates for Valentine's Day alone. Purdy's uses 260 litres of candy cream a day in the production of its chocolates in the two weeks preceding Valentine's Day.

The custom of giving gifts during the Valentine's Day feast is said to date back to the sixteenth century, with flowers becoming a tradition by the seventeenth. It is not clear when chocolate became a part of the feast, although Richard Cadbury, son to the founder, created the first heart-shaped box of candy shortly after introducing chocolate boxes to Britain in 1868. Since then, the Valentine's Day chocolate box, decorated in satin, lace, flowers, and ribbons, is one of the few occasions where the package makes as much of a statement as the contents inside.

The Ganongs are credited with bringing heart-shaped boxes of Valentine's Day candy to Canada in the 1930s. Jim Purcell, who became a Ganong company vice-president in the 1980s, made the promotion of Valentine boxes a personal mission. Later dubbed the Valentine King of Canada, Purcell would impress on the Ganong sales force that, "With all the hatred in the world today, it's nice to sell love."

A very romantic delivery truck.

# Section II

# Behind the Brands

*"When I was selling electronics you had a tough time getting appointments to see buyers and customers. With chocolates you never have that problem. When you call and say you're in the chocolate business they'll always see you because they know you're going to bring samples."*

Jim Ralph, President,
Rogers Chocolates

Sidney, British Columbia, is a picturesque seaside community nestled along the Saanich Peninsula on Vancouver Island. Located four kilometres from where the imposing B.C. Ferry discharges its cargo of passengers and motor vehicles before reloading for a return trip to the mainland, Sidney (also known as Sidney-by-the-Sea) is home to a treasure trove of charming boutiques, restaurants, and cafés.

Downtown Sidney has no fewer than ten independent bookshops clustered along and around Beacon Street, the community's main thoroughfare. Beacon Street is also a prominent address for several confectionery shops.

The Rogers' outlet, inside a renovated Victorian-style townhouse, is in keeping with the company's strategy of maintaining a presence in B.C.'s tourist destinations. Across the street is a cramped but cozy candy store, dispensing loose chocolates and sugar candy from glass cabinets and jars. Lunn's, a popular deli and café, has been selling its own line of individual chocolate creations since the 1920s.

In a crowded gift shop on the ferry back to the B.C. mainland, a small number of Denman Island chocolate bars are eclipsed by a larger selection of Kit Kat, Aero, Crispy Crunch, and Snickers.

Denman Island is one of the northern Gulf Islands in between Vancouver Island and the British Columbia mainland. Daniel and Ruth Terry moved there in 1994, hoping to start a market gardening business specializing in organic vegetables. Their early experience is reminiscent of the Ganong brothers more than a century earlier. Like the

Ganongs, who had moved to St. Stephen, New Brunswick, to open a small up-market grocery, the Terrys found the island already self-sufficient in homegrown and readily available organic produce. Undeterred, the couple decided to fall back on a second love: pure chocolate.

In 1998, the couple launched Denman Island Chocolate, producing seven varieties of forty-six-gram chocolate bars using organic Belgian dark chocolate combined with natural ingredients. The raspberries for Razzle Dazzle and the hazelnuts for Toasted Hazelnut come from British Columbia's Fraser Valley. Expresso Chunk (not recommended by the producer as a bedtime snack) uses "fair traded" coffee beans from Latin America. Six of Denman Island Chocolate's varieties use 55 percent cocoa mass. The seventh, Cocoa Loco, uses 70 percent cocoa mass.

Each bar is packaged in colourful tin foil and slipped into an identical rustic brown wrapper trimmed with green leaves and black script. The flavour of the bar is largely distinguished by the colour of the foil: orange for Zesty Orange, green for Cool Mint, etc.

A tour of Canada is a tour of niche candy products whose identities are constantly at risk by the national brands that dominate the candy counter: Purity's in Newfoundland, Ganong chocolate bars in eastern Canada (even though boxed selections remain a drugstore favourite from coast to coast), Purdy's in western Canada,

and Clodhoppers in Winnipeg, Manitoba.

Available in vanilla, chocolate, and peanut butter, Clodhoppers fudge, graham wafer, and cashew clusters are the brainchild of Chris Emery and Larry Finnson, using an old family recipe. It is perhaps wrong to characterize Clodhoppers as a local candy because in six short years Emery, Finnson, and the Krave Candy Company, which they started in 1996, have given Clodhoppers a national presence.

The candy has been the subject of reports in national newspapers, magazines, and networks, due in no small measure to smart marketing, including the Ben and Jerry homespun charm of Krave's two proprietors, Emery and Finnson (who prefer to be known as Chris and Larry, complete with caricatures).

Advertising meeting for Jersey Milk
(undated, but guessing by the style it is the late 1950s or early 1960s).

courtesy of National Archives of Canada

Finding creative ways to advertise chocolate to the public.

other approaches, such as broadening the appeal of a particular brand with new flavours and sizes, and copying the success of specialty coffee shops like Second Cup and Starbucks by encouraging consumers to cross the price threshold over to premium bars.

Both Nestlé and Mars have taken turns shaking the market up by tinkering with the natural advantage contained in their Smarties and M&M brands. Nestlé made news in Canada by replacing one of its two shades of brown Smarties with blue. In 1995, Mars ratcheted up the marketing by inviting Americans to vote on a new colour for its M&M plain and peanut chocolate and candy pellets. The choice was between red, blue, and purple. Blue was the undisputed leader, capturing 54 percent of the more than ten million votes cast. Two years later, Mars added green to the M&M mix.

Nestlé and Mars have also seasonalized Smarties and M&Ms with special packaging for Christmas and Valentine's Day, and, by using new production techniques first pioneered by Mars by imprinting the double M, they can add holiday icons to the candy. Not to be left behind, Hershey has created special foil-wrapped versions of its popular Kisses.

In the spring of 2001, for example, Dairy Queen launched the Clodhopper Blizzard nationally, following successful tests in western Canadian markets one year earlier. Still, despite their success, Clodhoppers remain a destination candy — an outsider against the national brands either manufactured in Canada or imported by the multinationals that now dominate the Canadian candy industry.

Not that the multinationals are immune from the struggle for market share. In the case of chocolate bars, a 1 percent increase in market share can add much more to the annual revenue. To tip the scales in favour of one candy line over another, manufacturers rely on a variety of tools.

Advertising and packaging are critical. But there are

Purdy's ads from the 1960s.

quick recipe

Take $2.00 to a Purdy's Shop. Ask for a one pound sampler box. Open it. And mmm-m-m-m . . . they're all ready to eat. Big, dark, luscious, hand-dipped Purdy's Chocolates. And with that wonderful kitchen-fresh aroma still upon them!

PLEASE DON'T EAT THIS AD.
TAKE IT TO A PURDY'S CHOCOLATE SHOP,
WHERE IT WILL HELP YOU IDENTIFY
OUR SMOOTH, RICH, WICKEDLY DELICIOUS
CHOCOLATES.

PURDY'S AT HARBOUR PARK SHOPPING CENTRE

Television advertising in Canada has been highlighted by memorable questions like "How do you like your coffee?" (Nestlé Coffee Crisp) and "Do you eat the red ones last?" (Nestlé Smarties); by a widely successful mystery, the Caramilk Secret (Cadbury Caramilk); and by one set of popular characters, M&M's Plain and Peanut, which began in the 1960s as crudely drawn cartoons, and which have since been elevated to computer-generated celebrity status. A female character was introduced in 1997 to promote the addition of green.

Along the way Canadians have learned "where the rainbow goes" (Hershey Pot of Gold), that "Life Savers have more flavours" (Kraft), and that "the only thing better than your Crispy Crunch is somebody else's" (Cadbury).

Following in the footsteps of Colonel Sanders (Kentucky Fried Chicken) and Victor Kiam (Remington Electric Razors), and before Dave Nichols (Loblaws' President's Choice and, later, his own brand of beer) and Dave Thomas (Wendy's), there was Whidden Ganong.

Every year before Christmas, the great-grandson and nephew of Ganong's founders would remind us that Ganong still hand dipped the almonds and that, while his boxed chocolate selections "may cost a little more, they're worth it."

courtesy of Ganong Bros., Ltd.

The laborious process of hand-dipping Ganong chocolates.

1966 press ad for After Eight chocolate mint candy.

Perhaps one of the most effective slogans to spill over from the U.S. was Hershey's "great American chocolate bar," even though, for the most part, Canadians couldn't abide the taste until the company reformulated the recipe.

In 1968, Cadbury first asked Canadians the famous question, "How do they get the caramel into the Cadbury Caramilk bar?" The television spot featured a drill penetrating a bar of Caramilk chocolate. Since then, the Cadbury Secret has been the subject of more than fifteen television commercials featuring historical and literary icons such as Leonardo de Vinci and the Mona Lisa, and Merlin the Magician.

According to the *National Post*, the Caramilk Secret is one of the most successful ads in Canadian history. Ian Bailey, a designer of new formulae for the confectionery industry, says he is asked the question about the Caramilk bar "more than any other question."

Eleanor Deacon, 1940. The fastest hand-dipper in the history of the Ganong company, she later married R. Whidden Ganong.

In addition to creating a mystique around the caramel bar, the campaign indirectly illustrated one of the traditions of candymaking: secrecy. Candymakers work with a limited number of ingredients. While the brand name can be protected under copyright, the actual recipe must remain a closely guarded secret.

"Anyone can read the ingredients on a Hershey bar. But to actually make a Hershey bar, you have to know a lot more than that," Hershey's Richard Zimmerman told author Joël Glenn Brenner.[12] As a result, a recipe for chocolate is as jealously guarded as those used for Coca-Cola or Kentucky Fried Chicken, and are often disclosed only on a need-to-know basis.

The process for making liquid-filled pockets of chocolate, however, is not much of a secret, nor is it exclusive to Cadbury. Neilson, for example, was also producing Treasures, a similar bar containing pockets of strawberry, caramel, and chocolate-flavoured liquid.

More recently, Cadbury has extended the Caramilk line to include a coffee as well as liquid chocolate version. It is part of an industry trend in chocolate production to leverage a brand with additional flavours and formats. Rowntree was an early pioneer with peppermint and orange varieties of its popular Aero bar. Nestlé has carried on the tradition with orange-flavoured Kit Kat and Coffee Crisp.

Given the popularity of flavoured coffees, the range of Coffee Crisp possibilities appears endless. Indeed, Nestlé has introduced a raspberry-flavoured Coffee Crisp. Can Irish Cream be far behind?

Cadbury has cross-branded its chocolate and soft drink businesses with an Orange Crush Crunchie. Hershey has introduced a peanut butter version of its popular "scrap" Eat-More bar, and a limited edition Oh Henry.

Prior to the 1990s, Mars M&Ms had been in a holding pattern. The original tubes of candy-coated chocolate that were popular with American GIs in the 1940s had grown into a baby-boom favourite in the 1950s. In 1954, Mars introduced M&M's Peanut. More than thirty years would pass before the company enhanced the M&M brand with peanut butter, almond, and crisp variations.

Likewise, Hershey has freshened its Glossette franchise (originally developed in Canada by Lowney) by adding chocolate-covered caramels to the brand. Despite the popularity of caramel, Mars has been slow to introduce a similar product to Canada, although it once did when M&M's were marketed in the U.K. and Canada under the brand name Treats. Similarly, Nestlé has not included an orange version of Smarties in Canada, even though orange essence has traditionally been added to the orange-coloured pellets in the UK.

The reason for new twists on familiar names is easy to understand. While a new product generates consumer excitement, it is also expensive. A new chocolate bar can cost a lot of money to develop and to build brand recognition through marketing and advertising. New varieties of

Short-lived generic candy bars.

established brands can achieve a similar result at a fraction of the cost. It also broadens the overall appeal of the brand.

And while taste is important, size increasingly matters. Nestlé has added chunky versions of its Aero and Kit Kat bars. In the United States, Hershey, which manufactures Kit Kat under license, has introduced a bag of bite-size Kit Kat similar to what the company has already done for its York Peppermint Pattie brand in Canada.

Still, no amount of packaging can protect a candymaker from a slip in consumer confidence. In 1976, Mars responded to public concern over a specific type of red food colouring by discontinuing red M&Ms. While the company did not use the food colouring in question, it claimed the action was necessary to "avoid consumer confusion." Red, which, along with yellow, was the original M&M spokes-candy, was returned to the bag in 1987.

Sometimes consumer outrage is self-created. In early 2001, Nestlé Canada inspired a consumer revolt when it announced that it would no longer segregate the manufacture of non-peanut and peanut-based chocolates. Despite the fact that 1.5 percent of Canadians have peanut/nut allergies, nut-based candies continue to grow in popularity

(although it is unlikely that a bar such as Crispy Crunch will ever return to the spot of the country's top-selling brand).

Nestlé said that it had considered dividing a single manufacturing plant into peanut and non-peanut operations, but could not guarantee a peanut-free processing environment. It is not known what Nestlé calculated the negative response from consumers to be, but it is clear that the company was not prepared for the thousands of letters, calls, and e-mails that poured into the Toronto headquarters.

Packaging for bars such as Aero, Kit Kat, and Smarties was already showing up with an allergy alert in advance of the planned January 2002 changeover. Nevertheless, three weeks after the company dropped its bombshell, Nestlé reversed its decision.

"We have been truly overwhelmed by the emotional chord that our original decision struck with consumers," Graham Lute, senior vice-president of Nestlé Canada, said.

In the final analysis, the reversal turned into something of a public relations coup for Nestlé Canada, showcasing a company that responded quickly to customer concerns. It was also somewhat ironic, since Nestlé was proposing a switch to a practice already carried out by its competitors.

# Consolidation

In 1947, the Canadian confectionery industry was rife with rumours that American food giant General Foods was about to invade the domestic market by purchasing the assets of William Neilson Ltd.

Morden Neilson, the founder's son and company president, had died from leukaemia in August 1946. His company paid tribute to its leader of twenty-two years by closing the Neilson booth at the Canadian National Exhibition's Food Building for a Saturday morning. At the time of his death, Neilson was the largest single shareholder in Canada's largest chocolate manufacturer.

He also appears to have been the last voice of resistance when it came to selling the business. Morden Neilson's executor, the National Trust Company, did not share the same sentiment.

Price controls had been removed and chocolate-makers had faced the scorn of consumers by immediately bumping up the price of a nickel bar to eight cents. Still, the industry remained unstable. Any company that could attach itself to the deep pockets of a foreign parent could emerge from a potential price war with a strong market advantage.

William Neilson Ltd. had already refused to enter a price pact, thinking (probably correctly) that it could undercut its competitors. National Trust thought it was time for the family to get out. But the assets would not go to General Foods.

In October 1947, the *Toronto Telegram* announced that George Weston Limited had purchased "one of the largest chocolate manufacturing firms in the world" for $4.5 million.

Weston was one of Canada's largest food processors and retailers, having purchased the Loblaws grocery store chain several months before acquiring Neilson. George Weston, the company's founder, had opened a bakery in 1882 — a few years before William Neilson had begun hand-cranking ice cream.

The company had its first taste of candy in 1928 when Garfield Weston, the founder's eldest son and current president, acquired William Patterson Limited, one of Canada's oldest confectioners and biscuit manufacturers, established in Brantford, Ontario, in 1863.

Neilson's sales conference (1954 or 1964).

percent of the value of shipments. Foreign ownership of the confectionery industry is also high. Approximately 60 percent of industry shipments are manufactured by foreign-controlled enterprises located in Canada.

In the early 1960s, inside talk of mergers and acquisitions had reached a fever pitch. Canada's major producers were experiencing a sales boom that even a new round of fluctuating sugar prices could not dissolve. Analysts were predicting that annual per capita consumption of domestically produced confectionery by Canadians would reach 14.5 pounds by 1966. While this remained stubbornly below consumption in the U.S., it represented an 18 percent increase over 1961.

But not everyone was sharing in the boom. Smaller family-run businesses were feeling the pinch caused by labour shortages, higher wages, increased transportation costs, and the enormous price of replacing outdated equipment.

Frank Covert, a former president of Moirs, described the situation. "One of the problems of labour-intensive industries in Nova Scotia is that their markets are too small, and unless they hook up with some big company, they will disappear."[13] In 1956, Moirs began an extensive, ten-year, $10-million modernization of its aging Halifax plant.

George Weston Limited had already been on a buying spree, purchasing McCormicks in London, Ontario, Paula Chambers Co. in Winnipeg, and Willa'rds in Toronto.

Ownership of Willa'rds passed from the founding Robertson family to Dominion Trust, then to the Blue Ribbon Company (where office staff were served Blue Ribbon tea each morning), to the Canadian Food Company (a holding company for Hunt's Bakery and Honey Dew), and finally to George Weston Limited in 1954. Willa'rds was merged with Neilson in 1970.

For years, Morden Neilson had politely rebuffed the efforts of Garfield Weston to purchase his ice cream and chocolate business, telling him that he "preferred to be a big fish in a little pond than a small fish in a big ocean."

While not as powerful as General Foods, Weston's purchase of Neilson gave the confectioner added financial muscle and a built-in national distribution network courtesy of its parent's distribution and retail businesses.

It was not the first example of consolidation in Canada's scattered confectionery industry (one of the most notable took place in 1925 when British-based Rowntree purchased the assets of Cowan), nor would be it the last.

In 1961, Canada had 194 confectionery plants, including 41 major producers. In 1997, the last year where statistics are available, the country had 106 plants ranging in size from one- or two-person seasonal operations to large production facilities employing up to a thousand people.

The Canadian confectionery industry is highly concentrated. The leading eight companies produce close to 87

A mountain of newly introduced thick Jersey Milk chocolate bars on display at an S.S. Kresge "five-and-ten" store in the late 1970s.

In 1964, Laura Secord bought out Smiles and Chuckles Ltd., and there was speculation that Sherbrooke's Walter M. Lowney — whose chocolate lines included Cherry Blossom and Glosette chocolate-covered raisins and peanuts — was up for sale. Lowney was attracting some unconventional suitors.

*The Financial Post* reported that Grace Line Inc., an ocean-going shipping concern, had been studying the Canadian confectionery market. Grace, which had already acquired the Dutch chocolate manufacturer Van Houten, was diversifying against the threat of increased competition from the airline industry.

Standard Brands (which would merge with Nabisco in 1981) was also interested in Lowney after making an earlier offer for Moirs. In 1967, the company assumed ownership of both companies. Faced with the rising cost of sugar and a $1 million loss, Moirs reluctantly agreed to the same deal that they had rejected only two years earlier.

1967 was Canada's Centennial Year. It was also the year that one of the most Canadian of all brand names — Laura Secord — moved south. The company was absorbed by Fanny Farmer, the Massachusetts-based chocolate maker and retailer that had been started by Laura Secord founder Frank O'Connor in 1919, duplicating his Canadian formula right down to the placement of a cameo on the boxes.

The takeover created a small uproar among nationalists. In Parliament, the acting leader of the Conservative opposition stood up and asked, "whether the government anticipates intervening in the proposed sale of a Canadian institution, Laura Secord candies, to a United States concern."

Laura Secord would not stay away for too long. In 1969, John Labatt Limited "liberated" 64 percent of the Canadian firm from its American parent as part of the brewer's diversification strategy. "And so the lady's safely home again," wrote Ernest Hillman in *Weekend Magazine* less than a year later.[14]

In 1972, another British candymaker set up shop in Canada. The impact that Trebor Sharps would have on the future of the Canadian sugar confectionery industry was not considered at the time, neither by Trebor's owners, the Marks family of England, nor by their Canadian business partners, the Leeds Candy Corporation of Montreal.

Trebor in England, like Leeds in Montreal, manufactured a selection of boiled and other individual wrapped candies, primarily for bulk sale.

Nor did the two partners think that the performance of the candy plant they built in Granby, Quebec, would later prompt the return to Canada of one of the world's largest chocolate manufacturers following a nine-year absence.

Laura Secord storefronts displaying loose and boxed chocolates.

In fact, the only thing on the mind of the owners of the new Trebor plant in 1972 was another round of increases in the price of sugar, and a shortage of experienced labour. By this time, the price of sugar had increased 2.5 times in the last three years.

Established players were also complaining about a 5 percent quota on confectionery imports to the United States, while British and European manufacturers of hard candies, toffees, etc., were "skimming off" 21 percent of the Canadian market.

For the first five years, Trebor added to market share through an aggressive acquisition strategy: Jean et Charles in 1973 and L.H. Bélanger (the largest manufacturer of St. Catherine toffee in Quebec) in 1974. One year later, the company added peppermints, sugar-coated Scotch mints, and coloured after dinner mints to its product line with the purchase of the Robert Watson Company in Toronto.

In the 1970s, Trebor would team up with the Woolco Department Store chain to introduce Pick 'n Mix, a popular concept that would help to revolutionize the way bulk candies were displayed and purchased in Canada. Pick 'n Mix would remove the candy from behind glass counters and put it out into the open. Carousels holding bins overflowing with tempting varieties of boiled candies, soft-centred licorice, eclairs, etc. would greet customers as they entered the store or left the check-out. Instead of a "candy clerk" scooping confections into a bag, customers would help themselves, often leaving the store with more than the one-pound bag of candy they would have normally requested over the counter.

Woolco (which would later become Wal-Mart), installed Pick 'n Mix carousels in each of its twenty-two stores. The concept was so popular that Trebor tested it in Detroit, but had to turn down a request from the A&P grocery chain because they were unable to supply carousels and stock for over two thousand stores in the time frame insisted on by the retailer.

In 1985, Trebor bought the assets of Penny Jane Candy in Montreal. Amidst the British invasion, the Hamilton-based Allan Candy Company remained curiously silent. Allan's lines of candy canes, wrapped Halloween Kisses, and lower grade Easter eggs and bunnies were so closely associated with Canadian holidays that the corporate logo consisted of the double letter "l"s in Allan forming rabbit ears.

Allan would not be silent for much longer. In 1987, the company bought out its thirty-seven-year neighbour and competitor, Dominion Candy. Allan had approximately six hundred lines of seasonal candy and was interested in spreading out sales over the entire calendar year. In September 1990, the company gained the rights to be the Canadian distributor for Score hockey, baseball, and football cards.

Five years later, Allan was back in the financial news, taking over both M&A, a joint venture the company had started in 1963 with Sweden's Malaco, and the Bortz Chocolate Company in Reading, Pennsylvania. "It's a way for us to get into the large U.S. market. Our existing sales there are nowhere where we'd like them to be. This purchase will speed the process up," an Allan spokesperson told the *Hamilton Spectator*.

In addition to its catalogue of low-cost chocolate, Bortz also produced candy canes in a variety of flavours including strawberry, blueberry, and pina colada.

Between Allan's purchase of Dominion Candy in 1987 and Bortz in 1992, its British competitor, Trebor, would itself become the target of an acquisition. In 1989, the U.K.-based Cadbury Schweppes Group took control of both Trebor and Bassetts, best known for its Licorice All-Sorts and cartoon logo of Bertie, a character made up entirely of the candy pieces.

Cadbury had left Canada in early 1987. Faced with the cost of upgrading an aging plant in Whitby, Ontario, Cadbury Schweppes decided to pull out, selling the Canadian licenses for bars such as Crunchie and Caramilk

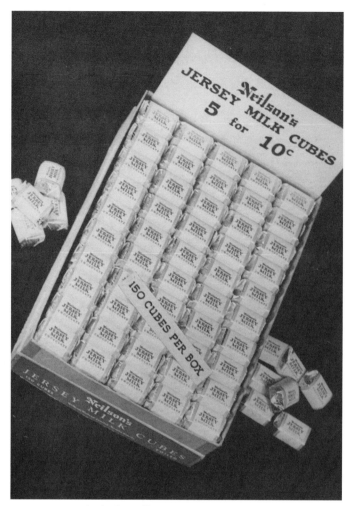

Early displays of bite-sized Jersey Milk Cubes.

for Neilson had mastered the famed secret decades earlier with the introduction of cream-filled bars such as Four Flavours, but the manufacture of Crunchie.

Cadbury had introduced the sponge toffee chocolate bar to the Canadian market years earlier. When the time came to move Cadbury's production lines from Whitby, Ontario, to the William Neilson plant in Toronto, there was concern that the aging Crunchie line would not survive the trip.

After talking with Cadbury production people in England, Australia, and South Africa, Neilson/Cadbury engineers set about designing a Canadian solution based on the best production techniques worldwide. As a result, the Canadian manufacture of Crunchie became the global standard.

Now Cadbury had stumbled back into Canada with the ownership of the Trebor plant in Granby, Quebec.

In the mid-1990s, William Neilson controlled 32 percent of the chocolate bar market, helped in part by Cadbury bars manufactured in Canada under license. In 1996, Cadbury reclaimed ownership of its Canadian franchise by purchasing Neilson from George Weston for $225 million. "It was nice to be part of a Canadian company, but one that was essentially a retail group," Arthur Soler, president of Neilson Cadbury told *Marketing Magazine*. "We are now part of a worldwide organization, with great technology resources and operating in 190 countries."

Analysts saw the deal as an opportunity to bring more chocolate bars into Canada, while plugging a major Canadian manufacturer into the global market. While the full-time return of Cadbury to the Canadian marketplace fulfilled both predictions, the larger outcome was the creation of a national giant in the convergence of chocolate and sugar.

While consolidation continued to shape the global market, some smaller Canadian firms such as Ganong in the east and Rogers' in the west chose to remain independent.

to Neilson. It marked the end of an era that had begun with a joint venture between Fry and Lowney in Montreal almost seventy years earlier.

Neilson's, whose Jersey Milk once competed aggressively against Cadbury's global Dairy Milk, continued to manufacture bars under the British company's name, using chocolate crumb shipped from Ireland.

At the time of the licensing agreement, one of Neilson's biggest challenges was not the legendary "Caramilk secret,"

"We've been approached by several multinationals," says Jim Ralph, president of Rogers' Chocolates.

Chocoladefabriken Lint & Sprüngli, manufacturers of the popular Lindor boxed chocolates and Lindt premium chocolate bars, took Rogers' by surprise in 1998 by purchasing San Francisco-based Ghirardelli Chocolate Company. Founded in 1852, Ghirardelli had a history, product line, and approach to sales similar to Rogers'.

But multinationals buying boutique firms does not always work. Ralph predicts that if Rogers' were to be consumed by a multinational, the first casualty would be the traditional hand wrapping of Victoria Creams in the trademark pink or brown houndstooth wax paper. "It's a signature for us. But it's also expensive and labour intensive. A lot of people would see no gain in hand wrapping," he notes.

Nestlé, which acquired Laura Secord's manufacturing and retail operation when it purchased the assets of Britain's Rowntree, sold the company to Chicago-based Archibald in June 1999 because owning and operating a chain of shops was not part of the Swiss-based food giant's core business strategy. Likewise, some industry watchers expect Nestlé's Wonka sugar confectionery division, which includes the former O'Pee Chee manufacturing plant in London, Ontario, to encounter a similar sell-off.

Nestlé is the world's largest food company, with a reputation for the smooth integration of even the most difficult acquisitions. Between 1985 and 2000 Nestlé went on a US$26 billion global shopping spree. Since 2001, the company has added another US$18 billion in assets and remains hungry for more. Nestlé is also about global brands such as Nescafe coffee, Perrier bottled water, and Kit Kat chocolate bars (although they are manufactured in the US under license by Hershey). Wonka remains a North American phenomenon that may not fit in the multinational's long-term strategy.

Nor has consolidation and globalization of several of the world's largest confectionery brands caused outward concern by some of Canada's niche players. Hershey's takeover of London, Ontario-based Leaf Confections is a case in point.

"There is nobody on earth I am happier to compete against than Hershey," says Paul Cherrie, vice-president of marketing for Concord Confections. "Provided we're not competing against them in their core business."

It is a matter of priorities. Compared to high-margin chocolate bars, bubble gum and gumballs do not even appear on Hershey's radar screen. "Bubble gum is small in dollar size and doesn't provide a big margin opportunity. Those are ingredients that will single-handedly chase any big chocolate manufacturer from concentrating on the category."

Greg Fash, vice-president of strategic marketing for Ganong, argues that market advantages still exist for independents even in an age where formerly great companies have been reduced to being part of a brand group.

"Being family owned and independent allows for more rapid decision-making and speed of converting ideas into action," Fash says. "Ganong's decision-making layer is one deep. A recent fruit snack concept is on store shelves today after very few months of being initiated."

That said, Ganong remains realistic. While several seasonal chocolate bars are sold throughout the country, the national battle for chocolate bar business against the larger multinationals has been over for some time.

"We have to pick our fights on the national stage," Fash adds. "We have opted to focus on boxed chocolates, fruit snacks and bagged confectionery as the core components of our range." Recent activity in the global confectionery industry suggests that several blockbuster mergers may still be on the horizon. And, while Canada will be nothing more than a sideline observer to world trends, it is unlikely that the country will escape further consolidation.

# Export Potential

How do New Yorkers like their coffee? Nestlé Canada is hoping the answer is "Crisp." In the fall of 2001 the company spent over half a million U.S. dollars to launch Coffee Crisp in New York by handing out over 500,000 bite-sized samples of the bar to passersby at several of the city's busiest intersections.

A similar exercise took place in Los Angeles several months later. But breaking into America's crowded US$12 billion chocolate bar market is no easy accomplishment, even with an accepted product and brand name that should stir Americans' passion for coffee.

Coffee is a US$18 billion a year business in the United States, with each of the country's 108 million coffee drinkers gulping down just over 3 cups a day. Perhaps Coffee Crisp's name oversells the product.

Anthony Imperiale, a panhandler outside Madison Square Garden, complained to the *Globe and Mail* that he could hardly detect the subtle coffee taste. It is a common observation. Nevertheless, Coffee Crisp, first created by the Canadian division of Britain's Rowntree in the 1930s, has a loyal following among Canadian ex-pats and some Americans.

Several years ago, John Flaig, a computer programmer from Milwaukee, organized an on-line petition to bring Coffee Crisp to the United States. Flaig was introduced to the bar during a visit to his grandmother in Winnipeg. He ended up getting inundated with emails, including a few angry messages from Nestlé telling him to stop "spamming" them. Each time someone submitted the form online, a copy of the petition automatically went to email addresses at Nestlé.

This is not the first time that Coffee Crisp has tried to break out of the Canadian marketplace. Rowntree introduced its distinct Canadian bar in England in 1961 to capture a larger share of Britain's growing chocolate biscuit market. "Everyone knew it would confront greater competition in the United Kingdom," wrote Robert Fitzgerald in his book, *Rowntree and the Marketing Revolution*.

Coffee Crisp, which never enjoyed a fraction of the marketing support Rowntree spent on the bar in Canada,

Stretching the toffee "crisp" for Crispy Crunch.

or lavished on Kit Kat in the United Kingdom, was withdrawn from Britain in 1965 alongside several other poor sellers. Similar attempts in the early 1960s to import the bar to the United States also fizzled.

William Neilson Ltd. was a participant in international trade shows as early as 1919. In the 1920s and 1930s,

Neilson chocolate bars were available throughout the British Empire. Morden Neilson, founder and son to the successor, however, resisted further attempts to increase exports, particularly to the United States.

Given the dominance of Hershey and the reluctance of larger firms like Cadbury and Rowntree to try to crack the American market, it is not clear how successful Neilson would have been. Neilson, however, showed no interest in trying, satisfying himself that the company was secure enough serving the domestic market. It appears that few rivals disagreed. Canada's small, disparate population meant that the Canadian confectionery industry lacked the productivity advantage of both American and European manufacturers.

As late as 1988, less than 12 percent of Canadian candy was manufactured for export. Meanwhile, one-quarter of Canadian consumption was supplied by imports. But it was not just disinterest that kept many domestic producers from competing overseas. In the 1950s, the Canadian confectionery industry struggled under unfavourable exchange rates and labour costs that were often one-half to two-thirds higher than offshore competitors.

The cost differential made exporters more competitive. By 1956, imports of confectionery items from Britain and Europe represented 14 percent of Canada's total production.

This has now changed. Since 1988, the trade deficit in confectionery has all but disappeared, as exports of Canadian confectionery soared by 390 percent between 1988 and 1997.

Globalization and consolidation has also helped. Hershey, which prior to 1995 never manufactured boxes of chocolates in the United States, now supplies the American market with Pot of Gold from its Halifax plant, once owned by Moirs.

Canadian confectioners are building a larger (albeit still a minority) presence at major global trade shows such as the International Sweets and Biscuits Fair (ISM) held every year in Cologne, Germany, and at the annual All Candy Expo in Chicago.

Why the sudden interest in foreign markets? There are several reasons, one of which is flat sales in several categories (including chocolate bars) in Canada. Overall, chocolate sales in Canada are stagnant, although the confectionery industry is experiencing double digit growth in boxed selections.

At the same time, the global integration of economies, liberalized trade, and multinational trade agreements such as NAFTA have caused large and medium-sized confectioners to adjust their focus outward. Eighty percent of Ce De Candy's two billion rolls of multicoloured Rockets (Smarties for the American market) are made at the company's Canadian plant in Newmarket, Ontario. Certainly Canada has some competitive advantages, particularly against the United States, where 95 percent of exported Canadian candy is shipped. Canadian candymakers purchase refined sugar at world prices that are typically 25 to 30 percent less than what manufacturers in the United States pay. Nobody anticipates the gap to be narrowed any time soon. The American sugar-growing lobby has succeeded in building a tight protective ring around its industry, supported by high import tariffs and special subsidies.

In 2000, American sugar-growers took action against a small Michigan-based firm that was importing a sugar-molasses syrup from Canada. The sugar industry claimed the Canadian company was making the mixture to sidestep American tariffs.

"American protectionism over sugar has been going on for generations," says Paul Cherrie, vice-president of marketing at Concord Confections. "It's mind-boggling that they haven't been able to tear it down. Nobody is happier about it than we are. But it runs contrary to everything that is philosophically American."

In contrast, the Canadian confectionery industry has been more successful in bringing the higher cost of dairy products in line with the United States. The Canadian Dairy Commission agreed to lower the purchase price of milk for companies producing chocolate for export and domestic consumption. Overnight, Canadian chocolatiers were on an equal playing field with their American competitors.

Chocolate makes up 63 percent of Canada's confectionery exports. One of the first Canadian companies to test overseas markets was Ganong. In the late 1980s, Hershey, through its Moirs subsidiary, and Rowntree, which owned Laura Secord, had approximately 70 percent of the boxed chocolate market. With a new plant under construction, Ganong had two choices: increase domestic market share for Delecto and other brands, or expand its universe.

"Whether [boxed chocolates are] at the premium end or the lower end, in blue boxes or pink boxes, with Japanese written on them or Scandinavian, we've got to find some markets outside Canada," David Ganong would say later.[15]

Advertisement for Ganong's Delecto boxed chocolates.

Japan was Ganong's first destination. In October 1988, the company shipped fifteen thousand pounds of Delecto to Japan, taking advantage of growth opportunities due to low Japanese consumption and recent reduction in tariffs to adjust the country's enormous trade surplus at the time. Within one year, Ganong had contracts in Japan for several container shipments.

William Neilson, who had all but abandoned the export market more than forty years earlier, was also looking at Asia. In late 1990, Neilson repackaged limited

quantities of its popular Mr. Big bar as Bang Bang for export to Taiwan.

This was not the first time that the wafer and nut bar had experienced a name change. Neilson had previously launched Denver to compete with Extra Good, a similar bar manufactured by Willa'rds. Following the merger of Neilson and Willa'rds in 1970, the expanded company began marketing the two bars under the Denver banner, with an Extra Good flash appearing on the wrapper. In 1977, the chocolate bar was relaunched as Mr. Big (and later promoted by hockey legend Wayne Gretzky).

In 1993, Neilson entered into a business relationship with Sabritas, a division of Pepsico International, to produce and distribute Crispy Crunch, Mr. Big, Malted Milk, and Jersey Milk under the company's Milch brand name. The four bars helped Sabritas capture 16 percent of the Mexican market within three years.

An attempt to launch Crispy Crunch in the United States, however, went sour. Neilson had entered into a joint marketing deal with a major American trading card producer. The same collapse of trading cards that paved the way for Concord Confections to purchase Fleer in 1998 from bankrupt Marvel ended Neilson's plans to export Crispy Crunch where it no doubt would have encountered stiff competition from Nestlé's Butterfinger.

Encouraged by his company's early success in Japan, David Ganong began taking a closer look at Asia. His strategy was twofold: to create new markets for Ganong products and to lower the cost of production by manufacturing some confections close to the source of raw materials.

While the bulk of Ganong manufacturing would remain at a new plant being built in St. Stephen, increased production costs were pushing the production of $1 million worth of mints, nougats, and the Yum coconut bar near the threshold where they would no longer be competitive.

Lower labour costs and close proximity to raw materials

courtesy of Ganong Bros., Ltd.

courtesy of Ganong Bros., Ltd.

David Ganong and family.

such as sugar, cocoa, and coconuts were key. In May 1988, Ganong signed an agreement with Thailand-based Rubia Industries to build a plant in Bangkok. The plant was equipped with machinery from the old St. Stephen plant.

The largest market for Ganong candies produced in Thailand continues to be Canada. For the first few years, 90 percent of the plant's volume was shipped back to St. Stephen. That number has been declining as sales in Asia increase with the introduction of new products tailored to local tastes.

By the mid-1990s, even Hershey was looking at exporting an Atlantic Canadian tradition south to the United States. Every year, Americans eat their way through US$1.2 billion worth of boxed chocolate. It is a crowded market, yet surprisingly under-served by American manufacturers. Only one company, Russell Stover Candies of Kansas City, Missouri, produced boxed chocolates for mid-income consumers.[16]

Hershey decided to test the market to see if there was room for one more mid-priced chocolate selection with a familiar American name stamped on the box. Florida grocery and drug stores were the first retailers to stock boxes of Hershey Pot of Gold — imported from Dartmouth, Nova Scotia — in Christmas 1995. By New Year's Eve, Hershey had its answer, and began making plans to take Pot of Gold national by the fall of 1996.

Pot of Gold is not the only Canadian brand in the Hershey arsenal that might appeal to American tastes. The purchase of Standard Brands' confectionery division in 1987 gave Hershey the rights to Cherry Blossom and the famous Eat-More scrap bar. Both products were developed by Boston-based Lowney for the Canadian market, and have enjoyed regional appeal. Hershey has also experienced mild success exporting Oh Henry Easter eggs to the United States. Canadian Oh Henry differs from the American version of the bar, produced by Nestlé.

Whatever the name of the next established Canadian chocolate bar to try and make it big in the United States, it is certain that its maker will confront the same barrier that prevents rivers of American chocolate flowing north to Canada: national tastes.

To qualify as a global brand a chocolate bar must have more than one percent of the market in more than five of the top twenty-five countries. Those that have include Kit Kat and Smarties (Nestlé), Snickers and M&Ms (Mars), Kinder (Ferrero), and Dairy Milk (Cadbury).

"There are virtually no global chocolate bars," insists John Bradley, vice-president of marketing for Cadbury Canada. Of the twenty-four chocolate bars Cadbury produces at its plant in Toronto, only four are exported — and only in small quantities.

In 1995, prior to the Cadbury purchase, Neilson Cadbury launched the Mr. Big bar in the United States, supported by an advertising campaign featuring basketball star Shaquille O'Neal.

Even if Cadbury did try to introduce more made-in-Canada chocolate bars to another country, the company would likely alter the recipe. This is not so with non-chocolate confections such as bubble gum.

The potential remains strong for gum exports. While the United States still consumes 83 percent of Canadian gum exports, Australia, Hong Kong, South Korea, Chile, and Europe are key markets. The French consume more chewing gum than any other population outside the United States.

There are also opportunities for Canadian confectioners to gain market share by responding to changing consumer demands, particularly in Western Europe, where gum remains one of the fastest growing categories.

Yet as attractive as making new inroads in Western Europe may be, Asia is the market where most of the production gains of the next twenty years lie.

Asia is massive in both population and geographic size. Nevertheless, the population eats less candy than any other market. Gains made during the mid-1990s were all but erased between 1996 and 1998 as a result of negative economic conditions. But several of Canada's candymakers believe the worst is over and the market will soon be unwrapping pieces of candy in record numbers.

Topping the list are Indonesia, South Korea, Thailand (where Ganong already operates a plant), and China.

China remains a bright spot for western candymakers because of its size, expanding economy, and currently low per capita consumption. Imports of candy to China have increased dramatically in recent years, in relation to the growing disposable incomes and general attraction to products that reflect Western culture.

Interestingly, today's China reflects the Canadian marketplace of the early 1900s, with an inefficient retail distribution system plagued by great distances and undeveloped roads and rail lines. China also has poor refrigeration systems that make it difficult to move chocolate.

Vietnam is considered to be another strong growth area, especially for chocolate. It is here that the makers of Canada's best-selling chocolate bars may be at a disadvantage. The three major chocolate manufacturers are multinationals that will either supply Asia from home or through branch plants. Both Cadbury and Nestlé supply Singapore and Hong Kong from facilities in Australia.

Niche and specialty products such as boxed chocolates are a different story, and may provide growth opportunities for Ganong, Rogers', and Hershey Canada.

Rising incomes and increased trade prospects under a potentially expanded NAFTA make Latin America another attractive market for Canadian confectionery products. There are notable growth opportunities in the Brazilian market for chocolate, the Chilean market for sugar confectionery, and the Colombian market for chewing gum.

Geographically, Brazil is the third largest country in the Americas, after Canada and the United States, and it has the second largest population. Recent positive trends for business include economic stability, reduced inflation, privatization, and freer trade. As the Brazilian economy moves forward, consumer demand for value-added products, including confectionery, is growing. The Brazilian chocolate products market is the largest and most dynamic in Latin America, and the sixth largest in the world.

# No to Low

In the summer of 1995, Neilson Cadbury launched Crispy Crunch Light — a low-calorie version of its seventy-two-year-old flagship peanut butter bar. The company was looking to cash in on the consumer trend toward healthy alternatives, a market being defined by low-fat salad dressings, diet pop, sugarless gum, and McDonald's puzzling McLean Deluxe hamburger (accompanied by a large order of fries and washed down with a Diet Coke).

Substituting the traditional Crispy Crunch red wrapper with a warmer shade of blue, Neilson began promoting its new bar through a series of equally light television spots featuring American actress Crystal Bernard, familiar to viewers as Helen Chappell on the hit comedy *Wings*. The series, which also starred Timothy Daly and Steven Webber, enjoyed another two seasons before NBC grounded it in 1997. Crispy Crunch Light was not so fortunate.

The first sign of trouble was in May 1996, when Neilson quietly altered the bar's formulation. Customers had been complaining about Crispy Crunch Light's bitter aftertaste, created by the use of aspartame in the recipe. Neilson replaced aspartame with Splenda, a calorie-free sugar derivative discovered in 1976 by British sugar refiner Tate & Lyle and researchers from London's Queen Elizabeth College. Distributed in Canada by Redpath Sugars, Splenda maintains more of its sugar-like taste.

Neilson's problem was the difficulty of announcing a new and improved bar less than a year after it had launched Crispy Crunch Light. The chocolate maker decided to reveal the reformulation to the retail trade, but say nothing publicly. "The people that are buying the product are liking it. It's only going to be a bonus to them," a Neilson spokesperson told *Marketing Magazine*.

On the surface, Neilson should have been onto a winner: a low-calorie version of a popular chocolate bar aimed at the growing trend among eighteen- to forty-nine-year-olds toward lighter products, including snack treats.

Certainly the evidence was on Neilson's side. In the United States, Nabisco's recently launched Snack Wells line of cookies, crackers, and candies were flying off of the shelves. M&M/Mars introduced Milky Way Lite, and Hershey came to market with Sweet Escapes, with 45 percent less fat than conventional candy. In November 1996, Hershey Canada added to the list of light chocolate bars with York Low Fat Peppermint Patties. Carol Hochu, then-president of the Confectionery Manufacturers Association of Canada, declared that Canadians were "clamoring for low-fat products."

Really? After an initial sales surge where low-fat products showed double-digit year-on-year growth, the market went flat. The problem was chemistry. Ingredients for reduced-fat products do not mix the same way traditional ingredients do. When it came to chocolate, customers, it turned out, were not prepared to sacrifice taste as well as calories the same way they will with diet pop or sugarless gum.

"Consumers have shown that they will not trade down on taste," one industry source told America's *CandyBUSINESS* magazine. It makes sense. According to NPD Group Canada, Inc., taste is the number one reason why Canadians like to snack.[17]

In the end, reformulation and a more targeted distribution strategy was not enough to save Crispy Crunch Light. Neilson eventually pulled the plug on the bar.

Crispy Crunch Light was not the first time that a Canadian chocolate maker tried to hook the market onto a healthy alternative bar. In 1933, Ganong introduced Sea Sun, a candy bar that the company claimed contained a tablespoon of cod liver oil. Despite good sales over the first four months, Sea Sun had to be withdrawn because the company could not specify exactly the amount of cod liver oil in each bar.

In November 2001, Connecticut-based Amerifit Nutrition introduced a new twist on Sea Sun: Vitaball, a gumball for children available in four flavours, each containing eleven essential vitamins in the gum base and candy coating.

Nor will today's reluctance for low-fat candy necessarily spell an end to the search. Kubata, a café specializing in chocolates, candies, and truffles in the heart of Toronto's Little Italy, is doing a thriving business marketing a line of in-store non-dairy truffles made from Belgian dark chocolate and organic soy beverage. They are not strictly vegan, because some pieces may contain refined sugar crystals.

As for mass-produced low-calorie chocolate, only 6 percent of the products Canadians eat are labelled low-fat or diet, meaning that chocolate manufacturers have some distance to travel. To be successful, the next generation of healthy alternative chocolate treats is going to have to replicate the taste and texture of conventional chocolate bars.

# Bars to Boxes

16

*"In this particular business it isn't the product that's lasting — it's the package. What Canadian home, after all, doesn't have a Laura Secord box somewhere in a drawer, in a cupboard, filled with buttons or bows or bills or love letters or just empty, waiting for some…?"*

Ernest Hillman
*Weekend Magazine*, May 28, 1970

It is the beginning of February. Only two weeks to go before Valentine's Day, and less than two months until Easter, depending on the calendar.

The pace is brisk behind the glass and dark wood trim counters of Canada's finest chocolatiers. Aproned sales staff gently insert delicate pieces of candy enrobed in rich dark or milk chocolate into heart-shaped boxes decorated with lace and ribbon. Grocery stores and drugstores — where the bulk of mass-produced boxed chocolates are sold — have also replaced Christmas selections with Valentine candy. Meanwhile, crates of boxed chocolates for Easter sit patiently on the shipping floor, waiting for the reds and pinks of an otherwise dull February to dissolve into the yellows and pastels of the upcoming spring.

Boxed chocolates account for 24 percent of industry sales. But it is concentrated. That two-month window between January's end and April's beginning is to the manufacturers and retailers of boxed chocolates what the summer season is to producers of Hollywood blockbusters.

By Easter Monday the boxed chocolate season is over except for a healthy surge for Mother's Day and a comparatively modest bump at Christmas. Halloween, the fifth big red-letter date on the confectionery calendar, is traditionally reserved for candy.

"Manufacturers of boxed chocolate — particularly at the high end — do 80 percent of their sales between Valentine's Day and Mother's Day," says Jordan Lebel, an assistance professor of marketing at Concordia University's John Molson School of Business in Montreal. "The rest of the year they typically eat their profits." Which is why chocolate boutiques

Boxed chocolate trade display featuring boxes for Christmas, Mother's Day, and Valentine's Day, 1950.

tend to spread out the peaks by stocking the shelves with biscuits, coffees, and other specialty items.

Clearly the box of chocolates has lost much of its early appeal as the gift of romance. Even a lavishly decorated box of Godiva truffles may reveal the unimaginative haste of an eleventh-hour shopper.

The erosion was inevitable and can likely be traced back to the 1950s, the birth of suburbia, and the expansion of

IDA Mother's Day display, 1938.

supermarkets. Until then, most chocolate boxes were purchased at a high-scale chocolatier or at the local drugstore.

Many Canadian manufacturers were content to keep it that way, fearing that by supplying grocery stores they would encounter reprisals from drugstores, particularly when promoting higher-priced boxes. In the early 1950s, Ganong's Delecto selection lost valuable market share because the company was slow to recognize the growing importance of supermarkets in establishing brands.

For the confectionery industry, boxed chocolates stir some of the most romantic images of candymaking. Legions of women dressed in white coveralls and hairnets, lovingly hand dipping candy centres to be tucked inside beautifully decorated boxes. Each piece a mouthwatering work of art. Each box an intended keepsake long after the candy had been consumed.

It was seldom like that. A one-degree shift in temperature can turn a pot of liquid chocolate into a solid, making dipping difficult. Likewise, temperature could play havoc on a day's work. "We always dreaded the real hot days, as we

Willa'rds Halloween retail brochure.

were sent home," said Jessie McIntosh, an employee of Neilson's Fancy Packaging division during the Depression.

Packaging could be just as stressful. "We sat on a chair with paper cups and boxes. A belt came along and we had to open the cups and put the chocolates in as fast as we could. Sometimes we were on what they called 'piece work' and got paid for each box. There was no talking, we were anxious to get the extra money," McIntosh added.

By the 1950s, most large chocolate companies had phased out hand dipping. Ganong was one exception. *Maclean's* described the added cost in its December 24, 1955 issue:

> Ganong is one of the last big confectionery concerns to cling to hand-dipping, a skill at which a girl doesn't become proficient for two years and at which she doesn't attain top speed

for five or six. An experienced dipper earns from fifty to sixty dollars a week. The Ganongs figure that an apprentice dipper ruins nearly a thousand dollars worth of chocolate and centres while she is learning.

Robotics has replaced hand dipping, giving Canadian manufacturers of boxed chocolates lower costs and greater volume to remain competitive, especially in the specialty export market. Still, producing boxed chocolate selections remains the most expensive and labour-intensive part of the chocolate industry — the main reason Neilson walked away from boxed chocolates in the early 1970s.

In Canada, packaging materials account for 23 percent of the cost of raw materials to produce and market chocolate — a virtual tie with cocoa. Boxed chocolates can soak up every penny, and more. In 1870, a French confectioner living in New York charged one of his customers $17.50 for the package, and only $5.00 for the contents.[18]

Boxed assortments are also a study in disparate consumer taste: women prefer caramel centres, while more men tend

courtesy of Ganong Bros., Ltd.

Coming off work, 1904.

The traditional chocolate hand-dipping department at Ganong, 1930.

The Ganong fudge department, 1938. Fudge was spread out on wooden tables and then cut by hand.

to enjoy syrupy chocolate-covered cherries. Quebeckers want soft, sweet centers, compared with hard centres, preferably with nuts, in the rest of the country.

Spending on boxes of chocolate also illustrates better than any other product the great divide between gourmet and mass-produced candy. The growth of retail gourmet candy shops such as Bernard Callebaut and Purdy's point to a consumer trend toward purchasing high-quality, specialty products at premium prices. It's a trend that one Canadian favourite almost missed entirely.

In 1972, Laura Secord was the largest candy retailer in Canada. The company had 214 stores and 440 licensed agencies coast to coast. But the last five years had been unstable ones for Laura Secord. Ownership changed twice: first to its onetime American sister company, Fanny Farmer, and then to John Labatt Limited.

Laura's travels would not end there. Rowntree purchased the company in 1983, and Laura Secord became one of the assets when Nestlé gobbled up the British confectioner five years later. Not one of the owners, beginning with Fanny Farmer, had experience in direct retailing of chocolate in Canada, and they all failed to spot a defined split in the marketplace toward high or low-priced boxes of

chocolate and away from the middle range. Laura Secord covered neither base.

Throughout the 1980s and early '90s, Laura Secord's distinct white-and-black-trimmed chocolate boxes with the trademark cameo lost ground in grocery, drug, and department stores to European imports such as Lindt, homegrown favourites such as Hershey's Pot of Gold, and American newcomer Russell Stover.

Russell Stover did not arrive in Canada until 1994, and had captured 15 percent of the boxed chocolate market in two years. Laura Secord's own tired-looking chain of white, Victorian-style retail outlets had not experienced a redesign since the 1970s, and appeared helpless to stop the bleeding.

An award-winning redesign and repackaging of chocolate boxes has helped close the gap between Laura Secord and rival shopping mall chocolate retailers. A marketing alliance with American greeting and gift giant Hallmark has put boxes of Laura Secord chocolate in many Hallmark stores across Canada. The two companies have also opened a chain of joint stores — an appropriate strategy, since most consumers buy Laura Secord chocolates to give as gifts.

In 1999, ownership of Canada's most famous chocolatier changed hands once again. Nestlé Canada, a subsidiary of the world's largest food producer, was never comfortable in its role as a retailer. The chain was sold to the Archibald Candy Corporation of Chicago.

Founded in 1920 by H. Teller Archibald, Laura Secord's latest owner is North America's largest retail confectioner, with 725 outlets including Laura Secord shops and Sweet Factory kiosks in Canada. The acquisition has also teamed Laura Secord with Fanny Farmer for the third time in both companies' illustrious history.

Canadian chocolatiers are preparing for another market shift as aging baby boomers develop an appreciation for darker, less sweet chocolate pieces manufactured in the style of European craftsmen.

It is good news for a chocolatier such as Bernard Callebaut, a chocolate artisan who has put Calgary on the world map. Callebaut arrived in the city in 1982, at the height of a recession helped by depressed world oil prices and the National Energy Program. It was an odd place and time to open a small chocolate shop specializing in hand-made European-style confections.

But chocolate runs through Callebaut's veins. His family once owned the Callebaut Chocolate Factory in Wieze, Belgium, selling the sixty-nine-year-old family business to Switzerland's Suchard Toblerone Group (now part of Kraft) in 1980. The factory continues to supply Callebaut with slabs of custom-made chocolate that the confectioner melts down and weaves into his own creations.

At Callebaut's factory outside Calgary, chocolate bars are manufactured alongside chocolate pieces using ingredients from Turkey, France, and Alberta. Callebaut's specialty is pralines, packaged in expensive paper and ribbon from France and Italy. Every year, he sells over 12 million of them.

In 1998, Bernard Callebaut became the first North American chocolatier to win the coveted Grand Prix International Artisan Chocolatier Award at the International Chocolate Festive in Roanne, France.

A final note about boxed chocolates: individual pieces may actually help restaurant wait staff increase their tips. According to David Strohmetz, a professor at New Jersey's Monmouth University, the presentation of candy may bump up a tip by up to 4 percent.

The professor and his research team conducted various experiments using different servers and a large collective of dining guests. Strohmetz reported his findings in the *Journal of Applied Social Psychology*: "A waitress working with the research team would offer each customer one piece of chocolate, or two pieces, or none at all when she brought the bill to the table." The results were quite astonishing.

It was found that diners who received no candy tipped about 19 percent, while those who received two pieces left an average 22 percent gratuity. Moreover, diners tended to be most generous, tipping on average 23 percent, when the waitress first offered one piece of chocolate and then, before she left the table, offered a second piece. Strohmetz's final conclusion … it is the amount of candy given to the customers as well as the manner in which it was offered that determined the level of generosity.

1940s automated box cutter for chocolate packaging.

# Wrapping and Packaging

**17**

**W**rapping and packaging candy is an important part of marketing to adults and children alike. The packaging of candy began in France in 1780. Chocolatiers wrapped their candy in elaborately decorated boxes featuring paintings, embossed plaques, and fine papers to separate the layers. Tins were first introduced at English railway stations to transport items such as boiled sweets.

Some of the class and kitsch of candy packaging in Canada includes a trend toward interactive packages by sugar candymakers to attract the critical four- to nine-year-old segment. As with boxed chocolates, the packaging of candy is critical. More than a printed name and guide to ingredients, the chocolate wrapper is the last frontier in the candymaker's attempt to attract the estimated 90 percent of consumers for whom a chocolate bar purchase remains an impulse buy. But sometimes even the best strategies can backfire.

In the early 1990s, William Neilson decided to give its premier bars a redesign. The Sweet Marie wrapper was changed from a yellow label with blue lettering to a bold back-and-blue label with yellow script. Products such as Malted Milk, Pep, Coconut, and the Cadbury Snack Bar were grouped under a new "blue" umbrella.

The wrappers were striking in appearance, but too much alike to create a distinct presence on the candy counter. Neilson soon returned to the drawing board, turning back the clock somewhat by giving old designs a facelift with some modern touches.

John Bradley, Cadbury Trebor Allan's vice-president of marketing, says consumers can expect shorter intervals between the tweaking or redesign of candy wrappers as manufacturers use new graphics and packaging techniques to keep the product looking fresh.

# Nostalgia and the Candy Store

*"Welcome to the world of custom-made Pez, family-pack Lik-m-aid Fun Dip and adult candy stores that stay open until 3 a.m."*

Canadian Business Magazine
August 1997

Candy, according to British writer Nicholas Whittaker is one of the first things a child will buy for himself. "Exchanging coin for candy is lesson one in the child's guide to consumerism," he wrote.

Growing up in the 1960s, no matter how well stocked the corner store was with Pixie Sticks, Pez dispensers, rounded Kerr suckers and boxes of Owl bubble gum cigars (in hideous hues of pink, yellow and turquoise), the selection was always better elsewhere.

For most of us it still is. Few drugstores or chain convenience stores can match the vast array of sugar treasures to be found in a dwindling number of mom-and-pop independents. The modern-day version of the old-fashioned candy store is something else entirely. Here, children can find candies in the latest interactive packaging, while parents satisfy their appetite for nostalgia.

We still call it penny candy — although it takes more pennies than once was the case to complete a purchase. That is because the penny candy culture is about more than candy. It is childhood memories of bike rides on lazy summer afternoons to invade the corner store in some distant neighbourhood.

Choice was worth the effort, even if the owner did occasionally "gyp" you on the price. And every group of children had at least one rogue consumer who would tuck a couple of extra pieces into his pocket on the flimsy excuse that the same owner had overcharged a nickel on the last visit.

From the New Brunswick general store of the late 1800s, with jars packed with colourful sticks of the finest Ganong peppermint, to the elegant glass and polished wood trim of the English-style sweet shoppes of Vancouver and Victoria, kids remain as much a part of the candy as sugar.

"Our market renews itself every five years as a new generation of kids starts to buy candy," says Paul Cherrie, vice-president of marketing for Concord Confections.

Children ages six to nine remain the prime market for Canada's confectionery industry. More recently, the market has both renewed and revived itself as adults return to the candy store. Retailers have been happy to oblige with retro-candy stores, the shelves and bins filled with every 1950's type of candy imaginable. Many pieces wrapped in traditional packaging (or as close to it as possible). And if that is not enough, there is the lingering aroma in the air, luring you to buy.

"The scent is powerful," admits Paul Cherrie. "It can transcend somebody from what age they are to a kid in seconds."

For those of us who grew up along border cities, the high energy candy store has been an invitation to buy those American candies not readily available in Canada, but whose commercials, beamed in from U.S. television stations in Buffalo, Seattle and elsewhere, were a constant tease. Good 'n Plenty anyone?

The market continues to evolve, and the demand for interactive candy and packaging that contains both sugar and play value has forced candy makers to replicate, in different versions, what Pez has been doing all along with candy dispensers depicting popular cultural items. In addition to dispensing more than 3 billion compressed sugar tablets a year in North America alone, the Pez dispenser, in its thousands of variations since the 1950s, has become a collector's item.

Tying candy brands to popular culture does not come without risk. There are complaints from retailers, for example, that by the time candymakers have rolled out a confectionery linked to the latest fad; the fad has already gone stale. It is for that reason that many established companies will use licensees as a promotional tool as opposed to launching new products.

The buying of candy has changed since the first wave of baby boomers became consumers. For one thing, packaging has turned the most unlikely destinations into mini-candy counters usually featuring bite-sized versions of traditional favourites enveloped in high energy wrapping.

It is the ultimate tribute to Milton Hershey, who wanted to package a chocolate bar that could break out of the traditional candy and drug store, and be available across every class of trade. As one Canadian marketer noted, "We have put candy into places you can't imagine."

Of course nostalgia is not exclusive to the retro-candy store. Higher end retailers such as Laura Secord, Rogers and Purdy's — along with the independent chocolate artisans — trade in their own version of nostalgia, showcasing their creations in glass cases housed in environments as culturally removed from the retro-candy store as the library is from the video arcade. As one American customer once wrote after visiting a Purdy's shop, it is like a piece of old England.

Among these retailers, Canada's most famous may once again be on the block. In April 2003, Archibald Candy announced it was considering selling Laura Secord less than five years after the Chicago-based candy manufacturer and retailer had bought the Canadian chocolatier from Nestlé. The 1999 purchase had escaped much of the nationalistic fervor that surrounded an earlier acquisition by an American firm. But in the final analysis, the 174 store Canadian chain was not a comfortable fit with the larger American retailer.

"I think the strategy process revealed that they might be better off focusing their efforts on the United States, where they haven't got huge penetration, as opposed to diluting their efforts in Canada," Tim Weichel, an Archibald executive vice-president responsible for Laura Secord told Canadian Press.

Archibald, whose holdings include Laura Secord's one-time American cousin, Fanny May, filed for bankruptcy protection in the United States in 2002. The company emerged from so-called Chapter 11 in November 2002, after closing two hundred U.S. outlets.

While Archibald is considering several strategic alternatives for Laura Secord, a direct sale is most likely. To who remains the question. Archibald has altered the Laura Secord retail strategy – largely for the good – putting more emphasis on its products as gift items while adding non-chocolate items to shield the company from the seasonal peaks and valleys of chocolate retailing. In doing so, the American parent has moved Laura Secord closer to the time when it was a purveyor of both fine chocolates and baked goods.

Several potential suitors come to mind: Cadbury Trebor Allan, which has slowly entered the retail field in Canada, or one of the western-Canadian independents who might seek larger retail presence in the east. Laura Secord also shares 18 locations in Canada with Hallmark Cards, although a purchase by the greeting card and gift retailer appears unlikely.

Certainly the sale of Laura Secord opens new opportunities for manufacturing given that the bulk of the company's inventory arrives from Archibald plants in the States. There may even be an opening to wrestle back some of the drug store shelf space that Laura has lost to Russell Stover. Whatever the outcome, Laura Secord will soon open a new chapter in candy making in Canada.

# Notes

1. Sophie D. Coe and Michael D. Coe. *The True History of Chocolate*. London: Thames & Hudson Ltd,. 1996. p 18.

2. Sophie D. Coe and Michael D. Coe. *The True History of Chocolate*. London: Thames & Hudson Ltd, 1996. p 165.

3. David Folster. *The Chocolate Ganongs of St. Stephen, New Brunswick*. Toronto: MacMillan of Canada, 1990. p 143

4. Cecil Maiden. "Hush-hush policy still retained by successor of chocolate maker." *Victoria Times Colonist*. December 8, 1951.

5. Felicia M. Wills and Julie L. McDowell. "Candy's a dandy process industry". *Today's Chemist at Work*. American Chemical Society. April 2001.

6. Adam Bryant. "Pow! The punches that left Marvel reeling". *The Sunday New York Times*. May 24, 1998.

7. Frank B. Edwards. "The magic of Rogers". *Equinox*. November 1, 1982.

8. It should be noted that the only known candy bar named after a sports figure was the Reggie Bar, for the New York Yankee's Reggie "Mr. October" Jackson. A Quebec company immortalized the number of Montreal Canadiens' great Guy Lafleur for a brief time in the 1970s with a Number Ten bar.

9. Yanick LeClerc. "The War of the Nickel Bar". *The Beaver*. February/March 1999. p 33.

10. *Financial Post*. Dec. 22, 1956.

11. Robert Fitzgerald. *Rowntree and the Marketing Revolution: 1862–1969*. Cambridge University Press. 1995.

12. The Emperors of Chocolate. Inside the Secret World of Hershey and Mars. Joël Glenn Brenner. Random House, New York. 1999.

13. Sherri Aikenhead. "Moirs Pot of Gold: Sweets for the shareholder". *Commercial News*. Undated.

14. Ernest Hillman. *Weekend Magazine*. May 28, 1970.

15. David Folster. *The Chocolate Ganongs of St. Stephen, New Brunswick*. Toronto: MacMillan of Canada, 1990. p 203.

16. Russelltover purchased rival Whitman Chocolates in 1993.

17. *Snack Track Canada*. Five months ending June 2000.

18. Wendy A. Woloson. *Refined Tastes: Sugar, Confectionery, and Consumers in Nineteenth-Century America*. The Johns Hopkins University Press, 2002. p 124.